D0858070

YALE STUDIES IN ENGLISH

Benjamin Christie Nangle · Editor

VOLUME 117

PUBLISHED ON
THE KINGSLEY TRUST ASSOCIATION
PUBLICATION FUND
ESTABLISHED BY
THE SCROLL AND KEY SOCIETY
OF YALE COLLEGE

POPE

AND THE HEROIC TRADITION

A CRITICAL STUDY OF HIS *ILIAD*

BY DOUGLAS KNIGHT

Assistant Professor of English, Yale University

NEW HAVEN: YALE UNIVERSITY PRESS

LONDON · GEOFFREY CUMBERLEGE · OXFORD UNIVERSITY PRESS

1951

For
CHARLOTTE R. STILLMAN

PREFACE

POPE REMARKED once to his friend Joseph Spence about the translation of Homer, "If I had not undertaken that work, I should certainly have writ an epic." This book is concerned with the implications of his statement, not as they grow from the expenditure of time to which he was certainly referring but as they grow equally from the expenditure of an important kind of poetic activity. His Homer has long been recognized, often by those most critical of it, as an original poem in many respects; my concern is with the three main sorts of order which underlie its originality.

Pope had a coherent view of Homer, and of poetry generally, which explains something of the motivation with which he approached his task of translation. In presenting his critical thought, Chapter I does not deal with its antecedents but rather with its specific implications for the writing of poetry, poetry which is at the same time a version of another poem. Pope's situation is, after all, a unique one; he is the only major English poet who spent twelve years of his life very largely in the study and translation of another poet's work. It is as a result important for our general understanding of his poetic achievement to know something of his attitude toward the traditions which, as he saw them, stemmed originally from Homer.

In terms of his critical thought Chapters II and III consider two major aspects of the translation itself: its local verbal achievements, the qualities which mark and define it line by line as we read; and its general or inclusive achievements, those which build toward an increasing coherence as we move through the whole action of the poem. The most striking quality of Pope's work as a translator is his equal interest in both these aspects of his poem, which emerges as no less different from Homer in its metaphysics than in its couplets. Chapter II interprets this "original" character of Pope's version in terms both of other writing, which provided him with a living heroic style, and of the qualities in his own poetry which could be shaped toward the demands of such a style. Chapter III uses the evidence of this style as a guide in understanding the nature of the translation as a whole, regarding it as a long poem which is both coherent in itself and heroic in the implications of its style and statement.

If one considers these qualities, furthermore, one must inevitably consider their relationship to the character of Homer's poem; this is a recurrent concern of the book in all three chapters. Interpretation of Pope's English poem is presented in the context of Homer's and of the heroic tradition which mediates between them. Pope's version is seen finally as an embodiment of many of the most significant qualities of that tradition.

My thanks are due to a number of friends and colleagues. Messrs. Louis L. Martz and William K. Wimsatt Jr. read an early version which was submitted to the Graduate School of Yale University in candidacy for the degree of Doctor of Philosophy. If there has been improvement since, it is often the direct result of their careful criticisms. Mr. John C. Pope read the manuscript in both its original and final forms and helped me greatly to understand my own purposes. Messrs. Cleanth Brooks, E. Talbot Donaldson, and Stanley T. Williams, as members of the Committee on the Yale Studies in English, gave generously of their time and counsel; and Mr. Benjamin C. Nangle, Editor of the Studies, advised me at many points about the text itself and at innumerable points about its proper preparation.

Mr. Maynard Mack first guided me to an interest in Pope and directed the dissertation on which this book is based. At every stage of its development he has been *magister severus, comis amicus.*

Saybrook College, Yale University
   February 11, 1951

CONTENTS

POPE AND THE HEROIC TRADITION

I

Tradition and Translation

I

SINCE THE APPEARANCE of its first four books, Pope's *Iliad* has been a cause of controversy. Addison's remark quoted to Pope at that time, "that your translation and Tickell's are both very well done, but that the latter has more of Homer," has been echoed in spirit by critics as divergent as Richard Bentley and Mark Van Doren.[1] And of course the claims for the poem have at times been equally determined. From Berkeley to Tillyard critics have given their respect to both its vigor and its serious purpose as translation.[2]

Bentley's variously quoted remark to Pope, that it was a very pretty poem but that he must not call it Homer, would of course not be important by itself if it were not used as a final and all-inclusive judgment of Pope's work.[3] Actually it seems to raise questions rather than settle them, and the same ones which have been more generally asked by most students of translation. What is the translator's responsibility to the specific poetic structure of his original? If he translates in verse, what is the proper relation between that verse and the "original" poetry of his own time? And what therefore is the proper relationship between the whole original poem and the whole completed translation?

The answer to such questions might seem at first a historical and relative one. Translators as different as Chapman, Pope, and T. E. Shaw have had audiences to acclaim the fidelity as well as the stimulus of their writing. Can we simply say that Homer varies from age to age, and so does the version? If we do so, I suspect that we are avoiding the real question of relationship. Homer's text remains the same; and while interpretations vary we must logically either find some common ground

---

1. For Addison's remark see a letter by John Gay of July 8, 1715; the pertinent sentences are reprinted in George Sherburn, *The Early Career of Alexander Pope* (Oxford, Clarendon Press, 1934), p. 144. One might set beside them Mark Van Doren, *John Dryden* (3d ed. New York, Henry Holt, 1946), p. 216.

2. Berkeley's attitude is made clear in a letter to Pope of July 7, 1715; see *The Works of Alexander Pope*, eds. W. Elwin and J. Courthope (London, 1871–89), IX, 3. Cf. E. M. W. Tillyard, *The English Epic Tradition* (London, H. Milford, 1936), p. 3; and J. A. K. Thomson, *The Classical Background of English Literature* (London, G. Allen and Unwin, 1948), p. 204.

3. James Henry Monk, *The Life of Richard Bentley, D.D.* (2d ed. London, 1833), II, 372, gives this version of Bentley's supposed criticism.

for them or give up altogether any attempt to judge either translation or original.

Perhaps another kind of statement will explain the variation equally well. Cowper objects to Pope's version as the height of artifice and finds Milton the exact English equivalent of Homer. Arnold agrees with Cowper about Pope but finds Milton the most un-Homeric of English writers. Lang, Leaf, and Myers feel that the King James Bible with variations offers a properly archaic and unsophisticated diction, while E. V. Rieu feels that the *Odyssey* is more a modern novel than a folk tale. In no case is it claimed that all of Homer has been presented in English; his work remains a center from which the translations radiate in various directions. For Chapman, Pope, or Rieu it is those qualities which can be brought into the translator's own particular culture which are most heavily emphasized; for Cowper or Lang, Leaf, and Myers the translator is chiefly responsible to a sense of difference between his world and Homer's. But in every case the variation of meaning from the complete *Iliad* or *Odyssey* is the result of questioning not so much what Homer means at a given point as what this meaning demands of an English writer.[4]

The theorists of translation seem prone to ask their question in a much more extreme form than the practitioners since they are not faced with the chastening experience of trying to put a complete poem from one language into another. As a result many of them perpetuate the hope that someday there will be a reproduction of Homer in our language. Arnold was supporting a form of this conviction in his essay, "On Translating Homer," when he remarked of a contemporary translator,

. . . when Mr. Newman says, "My aim is to retain every peculiarity of the original, to be *faithful,* exactly as is the case with the draughtsman of the Elgin Marbles;" their real judge only replies: "it may be so: reproduce then upon us, reproduce the effect of Homer, as a good copy reproduces the effect of the Elgin Marbles."[5]

Arnold's "real judge," of course, is the trained scholar who can combine his native awareness of English with a knowledge of the precise effect which Homer has upon him. The chief difficulty with this view is that no one has yet seen the translation which would fit the demands

4. It is important to remember that all English translators start at approximately the same distance from Homer's poem; no one of them can lay claim to an intimate contact with its cultural matrix, and each must find within his own world the attitude he is to adopt toward Homer's.

5. Matthew Arnold, *Essays in Criticism and Other Essays,* Oxford Standard Authors, p. 265. Arnold does not agree with his antagonist Newman about the possibility of reproducing each precise effect of the original, but he is convinced that one may have the over-all effect without the immediate one. As he puts it a few sentences earlier, the sensitive scholar "demands but one thing in a translation—that it shall, as nearly as possible, reproduce for him the *general effect* of Homer."

of such a judge. Arnold dismisses all of those which have been done prior to his time and presents in proof of what could be achieved a brief sample of hexameter which really begs the question of *English* poetry. The line and rhythm of the ideal poetic translation, the ideal reproduction, ought after all to be as indigenous as its language: and despite Arnold's assertion that there is no reason why dactylic hexameter should not be indigenous, it has remained a mere curiosity in English poetry. Since oddity is the last thing to be claimed for Homer's Greek, we shall perhaps have to admit that the translator's difficulties are even more extreme than Arnold saw them to be.

John Conington, indeed, has put the matter very plainly in an essay, "The English Translators of Virgil":

It is doubtless true, as a critical theory, that a translator ought to endeavour not only to say what his author has said, but to say it as he has said it. . . . every aspiring translator has been able to quote a long list of passages where Dryden has failed grossly, and has argued in consequence that a true translation of Virgil has yet to be made. Yet their case, as we venture to think, easily proved in theory, has uniformly broken down in practice. The fact is, that what they have proved has been proved not merely against Dryden, but against themselves. The question of fidelity of rendering, in the case of a writer like Virgil, can hardly be made one of degree. It is idle to discuss who has come nearest to the style and language of Virgil, when no one has come within any appreciable distance.[6]

Conington's concluding statement demands a certain amount of expansion, of course. No translation has come within an appreciable distance of reproducing the total impact of the *Aeneid,* but there are several which have done well with one or more aspects of the poem. And so with Homer; the Loeb edition's English gives one a good idea of his statement in a given page of the Greek, Rieu's rapid paragraphs give one a fine sense of the driving action of the *Odyssey,* and the Smith-Miller version of the *Iliad* provides an exact knowledge of what the dictionary sense of the words is. We can be certain that we are doing justice only if we recognize what we have a right to demand of some particular version.

As a result, the questions which we asked earlier in this section will admit of a variety of answers; there is no one thing to do with Homer's poem. As we have seen, however, there are certain positive conditions of English to be met if the translator aspires to do more than provide a page-by-page glossary for the original. When Johnson remarks, "The purpose of a writer is to be read . . . ,"[7] he is pointing to a most important consideration. As Arnold implies at several points, one must work with the language which is available; the reader has a right to demand

6. John Conington, *Miscellaneous Writings* (London, 1872), I, 167-9.
7. Samuel Johnson, *Lives of the English Poets,* ed. G. Birkbeck Hill (Oxford, Clarendon Press, 1905), III, 240.

that the translation he uses be truly readable, and it can be so only if it is in some way alive. It must maintain a consistent tone in English and in addition some ordered relation to the Greek.

As with the problem of what to expect in the "ideal" translation, it is dangerous to theorize about the proper English means for these two ends. Except for burlesque forms it seems unjustified, for example, to say that it is impossible to use any nonlyrical line or stanza in a successful translation of Homer.[8] We cannot detach the stanza form from the rest of the poet's practice, nor can we judge the success of that practice until we see it as a whole. As with the meaning of a given passage, it is fairer in terms of the impossibility of reproducing the original to wait and see what the English translator makes of his hopeless job. Only then can we know the ways in which his work is worth our interest.

In Pope's case this critical procedure has at times been used and at times avoided for a number of interesting reasons. Coleridge and Wordsworth's low opinion of his work is well known and quite understandable; it depends basically upon a change of attitude toward both the dominant style of English poetry and the relevance of Homer to the English cultural tradition.[9] Partially as a result of the objections of Coleridge and Wordsworth, however, more recent critics have at times overlooked the fact that they themselves were confusing an inherited judgment of Pope with a more general judgment of what a Homer translator might profitably do. Mark Van Doren, for example, remarks in comment on the ending of Dryden's version of the first book of the *Iliad*,

The closing scene with Vulcan is grandiosely convivial . . . Pope's rendering of the same scene is not half so lively; the laughter of his gods is imitation laughter, this is real. It is thinkable that a complete *Iliad* by the author of these lines would be, even now, the most Homeric thing in English.[1]

And Douglas Bush in comparing Dryden and Pope as *Iliad* translators asks, "In which version is the diction more simple and natural, the thought more unsophisticated, the movement more free and flowing?"[2]

8. Pope's use of the couplet in his Homer has of course always been a storm center; since John Dennis, critics have objected to it, and those like Arnold with some considerable sensitivity to poetry make a perfectly valid point about the difference between its movement and that of the hexameter. But to conclude that the couplet is therefore bad as a verse form for translating Homer overlooks the fact that in such rigorous terms we have no form which is adequate.

9. In a note to the *Biographia Literaria*, ed. J. Shawcross, Coleridge singles out the *Iliad* translation "as the main source of our pseudo-poetic diction . . ." (Oxford, Clarendon Press, 1907), i, 26 n. Cf. "Essay Supplementary to the 1815 *Preface*," *Wordsworth's Literary Criticism*, ed. N. C. Smith (London, H. Frowde, 1905), pp. 183, 185–6. As the Augustan idiom became more and more vitiated and as Homer became more and more "primitive," Pope's attitude to both lost its sanction; Coleridge and Wordsworth could not grant his assumptions and still do their own work.

1. Van Doren, *John Dryden*, p. 216.

2. Douglas Bush, *Mythology and the Romantic Tradition in English Poetry* (Cambridge, Harvard University Press, 1937), p. 18.

I am interested here, not primarily in the fact that Pope is objected to but rather in certain of the assumptions behind the objections. Both Bush and Van Doren take it for granted that poetic artifice is categorically bad; they do not consider the possible ways in which it might justify itself in a long poem, nor do they seem to consider the even more general possibility that all poetry is an artifice of some sort. As a result they can claim for Homer a complex of qualities which make Pope as a translator doubly unsatisfactory. Homer is natural and unsophisticated; he appeals to us directly, as Arnold suggested, rather than through the medium of a style.[3] Pope, on the other hand, not only is for such critics the height of artifice in himself but has imposed this artifice on Homer.

In terms of what I have just said about the difficulties of translation, it would be rather foolish to suggest that Pope's style and Homer's are not vastly different. But I think it important to recognize that this difference is inherent in the fact of translation rather than in the difference between a natural poet and an artificial one. Like Arnold, Bush at least is confusing an effect of great difference from our culture, which has always been recognized as one of the charms of the *Iliad*, with an observable fact about the poem's style. Certain of Homer's events are "natural," just like certain of Thomas Hardy's or Ernest Hemingway's; but none of these writers can avoid the problem of a style.

We may very well find Pope having difficulty with certain of Homer's natural scenes; but we must recognize that this difficulty is not peculiar to him—and also perhaps that it admits of no ideal solution in a culture different from Homer's. For the verbal difficulties of translation which we have been discussing are really part of a larger group of changes. Actually it is most difficult to make anything like an adequate translation precisely at those points where adequacy is most demanded—where the original poem is culturally most alien. For the simple nobility with which Homer talks about his kings and queens is an important part of what he is saying they mean; his style is one aspect of what he makes us understand about them, but we cannot think and therefore cannot talk about them the same way in English.

The poetic translator is in a doubly difficult position, then; for he must be constantly aware of the fusion of style and meaning in his original and constantly aware of the fact that just because it is a fusion he cannot reproduce it. At the same time, furthermore, he must remain aware of his duty to his own language; for he is claiming to shape it in such a way that it is somehow related to the original poem and at the same time related in a more complex way than that of the literal translation. It is this complexity of relation, ultimately, which restrains us from making any abstract and theoretical judgment about what a poetic translation

3. Arnold, *Essays,* p. 258.

should do. We are forced instead to consider rather carefully what it has done and then, with reference to the original, to note its virtues and defects as well as its independent interest. If an *Iliad* translation should turn out to be in no sense a heroic poem, it seems likely that it would be unsatisfactory in a number of other ways as well. But it might turn out to be a very different sort of heroic poem from its original and still have legitimate claims as a poetic translation. More specifically, in considering Pope we must ask what his translation is and try as far as possible to avoid judging it in terms of what it neither pretends to be nor could hope to be.

2

We shall be better able, I think, to work in the body of this book toward a fair estimate of Pope's *Iliad* if we first pay some small attention to its assumptions. By this I do not mean that Pope's statements of intent, or those of his contemporaries, should govern our judgment. But just as we are faced in Homer with an aspect of meaning which is permanently relevant and an aspect which shifts in the nature of its importance with the quality and kind of the reader's culture, so in considering Pope we meet attitudes to Homer which seem familiar and attitudes which are at first perhaps somewhat surprising and alien. We cannot really begin to locate his translation until we see where he placed the Greek *Iliad* and its influence.

Pope is conscious above all of two qualities in Homer, qualities which we can separate but which are not fully separable. The first of these is Homer's poetic power, as it constantly shows itself in the immediate and local effects of his work. "What he writes is of the most animated Nature imaginable; every thing moves, every thing lives, and is put in Action."[4] "*Aristotle* had reason to say, He was the only Poet who had found out *living Words*; there are in him more daring Figures and Metaphors than in any good Author whatever."[5]

The second quality upon which Pope laid great emphasis was the fact of Homer's "epicness." He was the greatest exemplar of a tradition still very much alive in Pope's time. Indeed, as W. P. Ker has put it,

The "Heroic Poem" is not commonly mentioned in histories of Europe as a matter of serious interest: yet from the days of Petrarch and Boccaccio to those of Dr. Johnson, and more especially from the sixteenth century onward, it was a subject that engaged some of the strongest intellects in the world . . . ; it was studied and discussed as fully and with as much thought as any of the problems by which the face of the the world was changed in those centuries.[6]

4. *The Iliad of Homer, Translated by Mr. Pope* (London, 1715), 1, Preface, B2^r in the Quarto edition.   5. *Pope's Iliad,* 1, C3^v.
6. *The Essays of John Dryden,* ed. W. P. Ker, (Oxford, Clarendon Press, 1926), 1, xvi.

Clearly the tradition would not have been so significant had it not been for Homer's poetic achievement.

> Be Homer's Works your Study and Delight,
> Read them by Day, and meditate by Night;
> Thence form your Judgement, thence your Maxims bring,
> And trace the Muses upward to their Spring.
> (*An Essay on Criticism*, 124–7)

But it would equally have failed of its full power if it had been conceived merely as the relation between one aspiring poet and one established one.

"For Pope, as for Milton and Dryden, the classical epic was no dead literary form, something brought to perfection by Homer and Virgil, and because perfected, therefore inimitable. No, it was a permanent ideal, which had indeed been worthily embodied by two authors of antiquity, which had perhaps been embodied by Tasso, but which could and should be embodied in the present age."[7] The fact of epic included Homer, for Pope it very definitely included Milton, and he himself might hope at least to be worthy of some form of acceptance by it.

This attitude is something a little different from the normal historical interpretation of epic. It is apparent to us, for example, that an elaborate tradition culminates in Homer; but that fact alone does not illuminate the relationship which Pope describes in the *Essay on Criticism*:

> When first young Maro in his boundless Mind
> A Work t'outlast immortal Rome designed,
> Perhaps he seem'd above the Critic's Law,
> And but from Nature's Fountains scorn'd to draw:
> But when t'examine ev'ry Part he came,
> Nature and Homer were, he found, the same.
> (130–5)

In identifying nature and Homer here Pope is pointing to the primacy of Homer in the heroic tradition conceived of as a cultural and artistic structure. The *Iliad* and *Odyssey* are available to us even without an accurate knowledge of the group of poems within which they may originally have stood. Their profound conventionality gives a superb illusion of independence.[8] And this illusion works finally because both poems have so consistent a relation to our deepest experience of the world—we agree with Pope in this—as well as to our sense of a valid form which poetry may take in exploring that experience. Pope, like Dryden or Milton, felt Homer worthy to dominate the heroic tradition, not for

7. Tillyard, *English Epic Tradition*, p. 3.
8. For an extremely rewarding discussion of conventionality and "originality," see C. M. Bowra, *Tradition and Design in the Iliad* (Oxford, Clarendon Press, 1930); Bowra is particularly helpful in his distinctions between the sources of *Iliad* language or action and their function in the completed poem.

chance historical reasons but for his power to make his expression so adequate a means of insight.

This quality gives Homer a rather complex position of guidance over later writers. It is evident that his achievement is a powerful force for their education. But at the same time, and in part because he gives the illusion of standing alone in that achievement, he serves as a strong check to their arrogance and insularity as well. As Pope said of the ancients in general,

> Oh may some Spark of your celestial Fire,
> The last, the meanest of your Sons inspire,
> (That on weak Wings, from far, pursues your Flights;
> Glows while he reads, but trembles as he writes)
> To teach vain Wits a Science little known,
> T'admire superior Sense, and doubt their own!
> (*An Essay on Criticism,* 195–200)

Perhaps we can understand such an attitude more clearly in the light of certain well-known interests of a critic like T. S. Eliot. His sense of the value of a continuing tradition in European literature depends upon two beliefs about the relation of past and present. The first he expresses as a concept of literary history:

. . . the historical sense involves a perception, not only of the pastness of the past, but of its presence; the historical sense compels a man to write not merely with his own generation in his bones, but with a feeling that the whole of the literature of Europe from Homer and within it the whole of the litera- ture of his own country has a simultaneous existence . . .[9]

The second belief exists as a particular attitude toward "the pastness of the past," which is implied throughout the long essay, "Dante," and per- haps appears most clearly in one of Eliot's conclusions there. One way to understand Dante, Eliot points out, is to know the kind of thing he read. "But such study is vain unless we have first made the conscious attempt, as difficult and hard as rebirth, to pass through the looking- glass into a world which is just as reasonable as our own. When we have done that, we begin to wonder whether the world of Dante is not both larger and more solid than our own."[1] This explicit recognition of the inevitable differences between one time and another is hardly the ap- proach of slavish imitation. It is rather a recognition of one's own partial- ness, an assertion similar to Pope's in *An Essay on Criticism* of the humility which must precede any adequate criticism.[2] Seen in this way

9. T. S. Eliot, "Tradition and the Individual Talent," *Selected Essays: 1917–1932* (New York, Harcourt Brace, 1932), p. 4.   1. Eliot, "Dante," *ibid.,* p. 236.
2.   Pride, where Wit fails, steps in to our Defence,
          And fills up all the mighty Void of Sense.
          If once right Reason drives that Cloud away,
          Truth breaks upon us with resistless Day.

a sense of the past is for both writers necessary for any true grasp of the present; it is the only way to an adequate knowledge of that world beyond him which the individual writer may then go on to modify.

In claiming this Eliot and Pope reject the spinal-shudder school of criticism; they assert that poetry is a matter of the whole man rather than merely of the nerve ends. If so, then poet and critic have a responsibility to attain as valid a wholeness as possible; and the tradition is a chief means of guarding against the inevitable vagaries of the individual, which make him partial as he becomes merely personal. If he is to consider the central rather than the eccentric, he cannot define that center in terms of himself; he must enter into some relation with others, a relation which usually grows through the discipline of trying to understand what they are really about.

When this relation between the individual and the tradition has been successfully assimilated, however, a further relationship develops. Homer's profound effect on Virgil and Milton really means that he has a part of his life in their poems. Though he gives the illusion of independence from what precedes him, he cannot be independent of what follows. As Eliot puts it,

. . . what happens when a new work of art is created is something that happens simultaneously to all the works of art which preceded it. The existing monuments form an ideal order among themselves, which is modified by the introduction of the new (the really new) work of art among them. The existing order is complete before the new work arrives; for order to persist after the supervention of novelty, the *whole* existing order must be, if ever so slightly, altered; and so the relations, proportions, values of each work of art toward the whole are readjusted; and this is conformity between the old and the new.[3]

The nature of the *Iliad* is only fully comprehensible to *Pope as poet,* then, in the light of the *Aeneid* and *Paradise Lost* as well as a dozen less significant modifications of the tradition. Pope as historian considers in his notes certain aspects of the *Iliad* quite independently of the tradition; but Pope as writer knows that its power is no longer separable from the poetic achievements which it underlies.

This general interdependence of authors in a tradition, then, is also an interdependence of the two aspects of Homer which, as we have seen, most profoundly impress Pope—his immediate poetic achievement and his epicness. As Pope sees Homer, it is largely because he was so enor-

Trust not yourself; but your Defects to know,
Make use of ev'ry Friend and ev'ry Foe.
(*Essay on Criticism,* 209–14)

Pope expresses a similar attitude in his *Iliad* annotation; see, for instance, his treatment of the Homer controversy of the moment: Bk. ix, n. iv; Bk. xi, n. xxxv; Bk. xxii, n. iii; Bk. xvi, n. xi.   3. Eliot, "Tradition and the Individual Talent," *Essays,* p. 5.

mously successful with the first of these that the second exists in European culture as the complex fact of heroic poetry. As a result Homer is not only the initiator of that fact but also in the most immediate terms a chief living part of it. *"Homer* not only appears the Inventor of Poetry, but excells all the Inventors of other Arts in this, that he has swallow'd up the Honour of those who succeeded him. What he has done admitted no Encrease, it only left room for Contraction or Regulation."[4] In Eliot's words again, Homer is "not only the pastness of the past, but its presence." He is like the crucial line in a sonnet, without which the whole would not exist and yet which has its own full meaning only because of that whole.

3

If such is Pope's general attitude to Homer, if "the permanent ideal" of epic dominates his thought, what are the specific terms in which that ideal is developed? The context of the translation can be adequately understood only if we know not merely that when Pope says "Homer" he implies Homer dominant in the tradition but also more precisely what he means when he calls Homer the greatest of poets. Our chief evidence lies in Pope's elaborate annotation as well as in his prefatory discussion of Homer's poetry. There he makes clear through his analysis of the *Iliad* what he thinks the chief qualities of a heroic poem should be at their best. I shall consider his interpretation under the various divisions which he creates for it in his preface, because the relationship between these divisions provides one of our clearest clues to the qualities he recognized as dominant in Homer.

The Fable

There is a certain ambiguity in the use of the word "fable" as a term of Augustan criticism;[5] but for our purposes it is far more important to see what was implied for Pope by fable, action, and design as a group of critical terms often interchanged than to worry over the extent to which he distinguishes between any two of them. As he makes clear in his Poetical Index, Pope felt that the central fable of an epic was the sequence of important actions which evoke for us the poem's "great Moral." In the *Iliad* this moral is, of course, "that *Concord, among Governours, is the preservation of States, and Discord the ruin of them.*"[6] It only finds expression, however, by means of a series of actions; it is not an explicit statement set up as the poem's justification but rather

4. *Pope's Iliad,* I, E1ᵛ.
5. See H. T. Swedenberg, Jr., *The Theory of the Epic in England 1650–1800* (Berkeley and Los Angeles, University of California Press, 1944), chap. VII.
6. *Pope's Iliad,* VI, 11 H1ʳ.

the result in the reader's mind of a particular ordering of events in the poem.

Though this is what the fable does, its precise nature is still not fully explained. As Pope describes it, "The *Probable Fable* is the Recital of such Actions as tho' they did not happen, yet might, in the common course of Nature: Or of such as tho' they did, become Fables by the additional Episodes and manner of telling them."[7] These two aspects of the "probable fable" depend of course—the first more directly than the second—upon the Aristotelian concept of artistic probability. Aristotle, it will be recalled, points out the wisdom of preferring in a poem the plot which could reasonably have happened over that which may actually have happened but remains an imaginatively improbable event. He feels that the exceptional is often a detriment to poetry, in part because it lessens the general and "typical" validity of the poem's meaning. This is of course a problem which can take many forms. In our own time, for example, the overly personal subject matter of certain poets causes them to run the constant risk of failing to communicate anything coherent to their readers. Being "out of the common course of Nature" they are also out of reach; both Pope and Aristotle are recommending a general availability in the poem's material.[8]

Such a recommendation leads Pope to his comment on the proper use of historical material in poetry, a comment which is directed toward the same problem of degrees of reality as that suggested in Aristotle's remarks about the sense in which poetry is truer than history.[9] Even if the historical event is reasonable and expected, it is still partial. It rarely implies judgment or expresses insight beyond its immediate, limited meaning. Just as no series of historical actions by themselves form an interpretation of history, so a work of art—if it makes use of actual incident—can only result from the imposition of the artist's formal ways of developing a generally valid meaning from such incident. As a result the artist in such a case must be concerned with "the additional Episodes and manner of telling them." The actual becomes the probable only by means of its precise development in the poem, and this fact brings us back to a clarification of "fable." Beyond the minor meanings of the word[1] and beyond the small differences between individual critics, its use points

7. *Ibid.,* 1, B3^r.

8. C. V. Deane, *Aspects of Eighteenth Century Nature Poetry* (Oxford, B. Blackwell, 1935), has a number of persuasive discussions of the relation between this interest in the norms of nature and the specific character of Augustan descriptive style. His book is particularly useful as an antidote against the assumption that a general interest in nature implies a failure in immediate perception of it.   9. Aristotle, *Poetics,* chap. IX.

1. Pope uses the same term in discussing two secondary aspects of the poem—its supposed allegorical ordering of "Secrets of Nature and Physical Philosophy" and its treatment (in what Pope calls the marvelous fable as opposed to the allegorical) of "whatever is supernatural, and especially the Machines of the Gods." See *Pope's Iliad,* 1, B4^{r-v}.

above all to the central achievement of a purposeful organization. It is this meaning which allows Pope to say of Homer,

It seem'd not enough to have taken in the whole Circle of Arts, and the whole Compass of Nature; all the inward Passions and Affections of Mankind to supply his Characters, and all the outward Forms and Images of Things for his Descriptions; but wanting yet an ampler Sphere to expatiate in, he open'd a new and boundless Walk for his Imagination, and created a World for himself in the Invention of *Fable*.[2]

The world of the poem becomes a structure of purpose and order only through its author's inventive perception of the actual. And the fable of the poem is this order in its most general aspect, the ordering of action.

Characters and Speeches

Pope is constantly fascinated by the individuality of Homer's characters. "Every one has something so singularly his own, that no Painter could have distinguish'd them more by their Features, than the Poet has by their Manners."[3] This does not mean merely that men of various positions and responsibilities appear true to type in the poem but that each one actually goes beyond the bare requirements of decorum and stands by himself.[4] He is both a certain kind of man and also one particular man. Odysseus and Nestor are wise and brave; but in each the mingling of qualities has its precise and personal form.

This precision is created by the actions of the characters, but also by their speeches. As Pope points out, *"Every thing in it* [the *Iliad*] *has Manners* (as *Aristotle* expresses it) that is, every thing is acted or spoken. It is hardly credible in a Work of such length, how small a Number of Lines are employ'd in Narration."[5] The poem acquires part of its power through maintaining in its people the illusion that we are in contact with a world rather than a poet.

The propriety or decorum of the chief characters, then, can be defined only in terms of the mutual dependence of action and speech. This is a far simpler type of presentation, in certain ways, than the methods of developing character with which we are familiar at the moment. It is useful to remember, however, in describing Pope's attitude toward

---

2. *Ibid.*, B3ʳ.   3. *Ibid.*, C1ʳ.
4. The common Renaissance and Augustan idea of decorum is well known; it seems to have consisted above all in making sure that one's kings and cowherds never violated their stations. As Thomas Rymer says in his analysis of *The Maid's Tragedy*, "If it be said that the King was accessary to the falsehood, I question whether in Poetry a King can be an accessary to a crime . . ." "Tragedies of the Last Age," *Seventeenth Century Critical Essays*, ed. J. E. Spingarn (Oxford, Clarendon Press, 1908), II, 195. Pope's attitude toward character has little to do with such oversimplification; he is interested in the power of poetry to evoke the individual, not to suppress it, while he recognizes that the evocation must fit the poem as a whole. For further examples of the conventional critical attitude, see Swedenberg, *Theory of Epic*, pp. 23-4.
5. *Pope's Iliad*, I, C2ʳ.

Homer's characters that Homer's concern is with the individual in an objective context rather than in the subjective context often created by Proust or Joyce. And the additional fact that the poet as a person is so concealed in the *Iliad* also helps to direct our emphasis toward the characters in their cosmos; Homer's similes and the superworld of his gods create this cosmos in his poem as a parallel to what Proust's social memory provides for *À La Recherche du temps perdu*—a structure within which our judgment of the action may develop. And because the poem provides this objectified world for its action, we do not require the enormous evocation of detail necessary when the context grows from the characters rather than existing beyond them.

Pope considers the *Iliad*'s characters in this context by what may at first seem the abstract method of relating them to the moral as he understands it. He remarks about Achilles,

We should know that the Poet has rather study'd Nature than Perfection in the laying down his Characters. He resolv'd to sing the Consequences of Anger; he consider'd what Virtues and Vices would conduce most to bring his Moral out of the Fable; and artfully dispos'd them in his chief Persons . . . Thus he has plac'd Pride with Magnanimity in *Agamemnon,* and Craft with Prudence in *Ulysses*. And thus we must take his *Achilles* . . . as one compounded of Courage and Anger; one who finds himself almost invincible, and assumes an uncontroul'd Carriage upon the Self-consciousness of his Worth; whose high Strain of Honour will not suffer him to betray his Friends or fight against them . . . but whose inexorable Resentment will not let him hearken to any Terms of Accommodation. These are the Lights and Shades of his Character, which *Homer* has heighten'd and darkned in Extreams; because on the one side Valour is the darling Quality of Epic Poetry, and on the other, Anger the particular Subject of his Poem.[6]

In explaining why Achilles is exaggerated, Pope is pointing to a necessity of all dramatic poetry. The illusion of truth is given to us by something which is completely nonfaithful if directly translated into our world. Lear and Othello are just as unreal as Achilles; but in all three cases there is an exaggeration which turns out to be the only means of penetrating to realities so basic that they are not available in individual fleshly lives.

At the same time we notice in the passage that the abstractions—Courage, Anger, or Magnanimity—are an introduction to a highly specific if not realistic consideration of character. A striking example of that awareness which at some point in the notes Pope shows for most of the chief actors is his presentation of Idomeneus.

Idomeneus appears at large in this Book, whose Character (if I take it right) is such as we see pretty often in common Life: A Person of the first Rank, sufficient enough of his high Birth, growing into Years, conscious of his Decline in Strength and active Qualities; and therefore endeavouring to make it up to himself in Dignity, and to preserve the Veneration of others. The true

6. *Ibid.*, Bk. I, n. xxiii.

Picture of a stiff old Soldier, not willing to lose any of the Reputation he has acquir'd; yet not inconsiderate in Danger; but by the Sense of his Age, and by his Experience in Battel, become too cautious to engage with any great odds against him: Very careful and tender of his Soldiers, whom he had commanded so long that they were become old Acquaintance; (so that it was with great Judgement *Homer* chose to introduce him here, in performing a kind Office to one of 'em who was wounded.) Talkative upon Subjects of War, as afraid that others might lose the Memory of what he had done in better Days . . . One may observe some Strokes of Lordliness and State in his Character . . . The Vaunting of his Family in this Book, together with his Sarcasms and contemptuous Railleries on his dead Enemies, savour of the same Turn of Mind.[7]

The most important thing about this development of Idomeneus is its doubleness; while he is clearly set apart as a personality, just as clearly he is described by Pope as a character with an integral relation to the onward movement of the poem. We cannot completely detach him for separate contemplation, and it would be from many points of view a rather damning criticism of the *Iliad* if we could. As Pope sees it, Homer is concerned with the individuality of Idomeneus *as an actor,* not as the representative of a mental state sufficiently specialized to be called "individual." (The *Iliad* contrasts greatly with a verse-novel like *The Ring and the Book,* where the characters exist separately and for themselves. They are included in a plot rather than an action—there is no development in the piece—and they provide its only significance, rather than participating in a total meaning which is created from a variety of other elements in addition to their personalities.)

In directing his own and the reader's attention to the disciplined character treatment in the *Iliad,* Pope is conscious of the same achievement which he felt so important in Homer's handling of fable. The characters are presented within a context of purpose. Like ourselves, they have parts to play; and the emphasis of the poem is on the way in which they succeed or fail with the action demanded of them. They are not realistic in the amount of detail which we learn about them; but like the fable which they implement, they deal constantly with the actual at the point of its most general significance.

Sentiments

A comparable sense of purpose is present for Pope in Homer's "Sentiments." In describing them he speaks rather cryptically about "the Sublimity and Spirit of his Thoughts,"[8] but a clue to this aspect of Pope's feeling for Homer may be found in one of his borrowed remarks about Virgil: "the *Roman* Author seldom rises into very astonishing Senti-

7. *Ibid.,* Bk. xiii, n. xix; and cf. the development of Agamemnon in Bk. xi, n. i.
8. *Ibid.,* i, C2ᵛ.

ments where he is not fired by the *Iliad.*"⁹ By his interpretations of the action of the poem, Homer makes us see the world in a new way, as Virgil seldom does. Something of the same sort of individuality which we have seen in Homer's characters also gives freshness to his observations about the cosmos in which those characters move, and their relation to it.

This freshness is not described by Pope as originality in the shallow sense; Homer is not presenting us with eccentric observation. His view of nature and society is not—like that of Poe or Baudelaire at times— so special that it bears no relation to our experience. For Pope Homer presents his *sententiae* as part of a larger action in which the explicit statement participates to form some new total insight. It is such an interpretation which suggests his remark about a famous speech of Apollo's in Book xxi, "The Poet is very happy in interspersing his Poem with moral Sentences; in this place he steals away his Reader from War and Horror, and gives him a beautiful Admonition of his own Frailty. 'Shall I (says *Apollo*) contend with thee for the sake of Man? Man, who is no more than a Leaf of a Tree, now green and flourishing, but soon wither'd away and gone?' "¹ Here Apollo's sentiment is functional in the poem as a contrast to the carnage which has preceded and which will reach its climax in the single death of Hector. The mortality of man may take many forms; and Apollo's remark brings out the irony of war as a humanly determined hastening of an inevitable end. Removed from such a context, his statement would be neither so sublime nor so spirited. Pope remarks of another passage,

The Poet in this Image of an Inundation, takes occasion to mention a Sentiment of great Piety, that such Calamities were the Effects of divine Justice punishing the Sins of Mankind. This might probably refer to the Tradition of an universal Deluge, which was very common among the ancient heathen Writers; most of them ascribing the Cause of this Deluge to the Wrath of Heaven provoked by the Wickedness of Men . . . This is one, among a thousand Instances, of *Homer*'s indirect and oblique manner of introducing moral Sentences and Instructions. These agreeably break in upon his Reader even in Descriptions and poetical Parts, where one naturally expects only Painting and Amusement.²

The lessons by which we profit are never out of place as poetry, then; and although they may be detached by the reader from their context they have their most significant place within it and extending it. They are a part of the sense of inclusiveness—the illusion of omniscient wisdom— which seems to be permanently characteristic of the effect of the *Iliad.* That they can be absorbed so completely is, as Pope implies in his remark about "Painting and Amusement," almost a final test of the poem's dramatic power; its ideas as well as its people are parts of one whole—

9. *Ibid.*   1. *Ibid.,* Bk. xxi, n. xxvi.
2. *Ibid.,* Bk. xvi, n. xxxiii.

the whole to which they contribute and from which in turn they derive meaning.

Descriptions, Images, and Similes

The dramatic, however, is only one part of the task of the heroic poet. Pope says of Homer's descriptive power that

. . . all things, in their various Views, presented themselves in an Instant, and had their Impressions taken off to Perfection at a Heat. Nay, he not only gives us the full Prospects of Things, but several unexpected Peculiarities and Side-Views, unobserv'd by any Painter but *Homer*. Nothing is so surprizing as the Descriptions of his Battels, which take up no less than half the *Iliad,* and are supply'd with so vast a Variety of Incidents, that no one bears a Likeness to another; such different Kinds of Deaths, that no two Heroes are wounded in the same manner; and such a Profusion of noble Ideas, that every Battel rises above the last in Greatness, Horror, and Confusion.[3]

Here we actually see Pope exploring that sense of limitless and yet comprehensible suffering which is the greatest descriptive achievement of the *Iliad.* He finds in the descriptions a range of power parallel to that in other aspects of the poem; Homer is able to make an immense variety of observation and experience work together to confirm our awareness that the struggle of the *Iliad* is a world conflict. We feel—as with his *sententiae*—that he goes to the heart of human experience even while he extends its usual limits. He gives us "the full Prospects of Things," while at the same time he can help us to see that they are not merely what we had always assumed. In this way Homer meets the standard which Johnson set up in discussing the metaphysical poets; the *Iliad* affects us "as Wit which is at once natural and new, that which though not obvious is, upon its first production, acknowledged to be just; . . . that, which he that never found it wonders how he missed."[4]

From his notes we can see that the images and similes occupy for Pope a place of equal importance with the descriptions in implementing Homer's inclusive and yet inevitably selective treatment of reality, his particular use of it in the creation of a cosmos for the *Iliad.* As Pope remarks of the famous bee simile in the second book,

This is the first Simile in *Homer,* and we may observe in general that he excels all Mankind in the Number, Variety, and Beauty of his Comparisons. . . . The beauty of *Homer*'s [image of the bees] is not inferior to *Virgil*'s, if we consider with what Exactness it answers to its end. It consists of three Particulars; the vast Number of the Troops is exprest in the Swarms, their tumultuous manner of issuing out of the Ships, and the perpetual Egression

---

3. *Ibid.,* I, C2ᵛ–C3ʳ.

4. Johnson, *Lives of the Poets,* I, 20. Pope often speaks in his notes of this revelatory power in Homer's descriptions; particularly striking in the earlier part of the poem are Bk. II, n. vii; Bk. IV, n. xi; Bk. VII, n. xviii; and Bk. x, n. viii.

which seem'd without end, are imaged in the Bees pouring out of the Rock; and lastly their Dispersion over all the Shore, in their descending on the Flowers in the Vales.[5]

The first end which Pope mentions here is that of conformity between image and subject, and he implies also the value for the poem of such conformity. It lies in the particular awareness of the army which we can receive only through the image—a sense of multitude and mass, and a great variety of activities. These are in turn combined so as to give us an increased consciousness of the way in which a mob of men operates, and within that general consciousness a knowledge of the blind, instinctive way in which armies are to sway back and forth throughout the whole *Iliad*.[6]

The point for Pope about all these aspects of language is that they are functional. We apprehend something by means of them which we would not otherwise grasp in its completeness. When we see an object or event in one of these passages, its vividness is an insight into something beyond the object as well. It is in fact the job of description and simile not merely to evoke but to create that insight, to fuse image and wisdom as the poem's characters, for instance, fuse individual men with an understanding of man.

Expression and Versification

Pope finds this same creative achievement in another aspect of Homer's language. He is constantly dazzled by "that Harmony, which makes us confess he had not only the richest Head, but the finest Ear in the World."[7] And the great result of that harmony for Homer was that "his Measures, instead of being Fetters to his Sense, were always in readiness to run along with the Warmth of his Rapture; and even to give a farther Representation of his Notions, in the Correspondence of their Sounds to what they signify'd."[8]

Without embroiling ourselves in the whole controversy about sound and sense, we have a right to ask whether the attitude of Pope and many others does not have more to recommend it than Dr. Johnson, say, was willing to grant. Of course Johnson had a particular group of very real

5. *Pope's Iliad*, Bk. ɪɪ, n. vi.
6. Most of Homer's extended similes receive equally extensive treatment in the notes: Bk. vɪɪɪ, n. xxxiv, the famous comparison of Gorgythio to a drooping poppy; Bk. xɪɪɪ, n. xviii, Hector dropping from the wall like a rock forced on by a mountain stream; and Bk. xvɪ, n. xix, the Myrmidons going out to battle like wolves,—are among Pope's best discussions of the range both of immediate excitement and development of the main action brought to the poem by them.   7. *Pope's Iliad*, ɪ, C4ᵛ.
8. *Ibid*. Pope is constantly preoccupied with the sound-sense relationship. His tour de force treatment of the subject in *An Essay on Criticism* is well known; perhaps his clearest exposition of "a style of sound," as he calls it, is in a letter originally to Henry Cromwell but printed in a revised form as though written to William Walsh. See *The Works of Alexander Pope*, ed. Elwin and Courthope, vɪ, 56 ff., 111 ff.

offenders in mind. "This notion of representative metre," he remarks in the *Life of Pope,* "and the desire of discovering frequent adaptations of the sound to the sense, have produced, in my opinion, many wild conceits and imaginary beauties. All that can furnish this representation are the sounds of the words considered singly, and the time in which they are pronounced."[9] Johnson seems to be protesting against those who fancy that sound apart from meaning can convey a particular attitude or event. Pope never makes such an extravagant claim, however; he seems rather to feel, as John Conington remarked in protest against Johnson, "that a poet is not bound to produce a line where the sound of the words shall tell its own tale quite irrespectively of the sense, but only one where the sound will assist the impression which the sense is already making."[1]

When Pope calls this power a "style of sound," as he does in his well-known letter to Walsh, he is really saying that the precise way in which something is done has the most important kind of effect on what it is that is ultimately done. Virgil's *Georgics* are a superb example of this puzzle of style in its general sense; one cannot talk adequately about them without realizing that Virgil's dignified treatment of a rustic world is a basic part of what he is saying about the importance of that world— and about the relation to it of other worlds never made explicit in the *Georgics.*[2] In exactly the same way a style of sound in Homer can guide us to what a given passage is about.[3]

9. Johnson, *Lives of the Poets,* III, 230.

1. Conington, *Writings,* I, 24. For an extremely brief but sensible discussion of the relationship between sound and meaning see C. M. Lotspeich, "The Metrical Technique of Pope's Illustrative Couplets," *Journal of English and Germanic Philology, 26* (1927), 471–4. At the opposite extreme from Johnson are such books as C. F. Jacob, *The Foundations and Nature of Verse* (New York, Columbia University Press, 1918), and K. M. Wilson, *Sound and Meaning in English Poetry* (London and Toronto, Jonathan Cape, 1930), especially in Bk. II, chap. I.

2. See C. N. Cochrane, *Christianity and Classical Culture* (Oxford, Clarendon Press, 1940), p. 65; what the *Georgics* suggests "is not sentimental rapture but a call to work . . . as though the finest product of a country were the men she breeds."

3. One of the best examples of Pope's own interest in this quality is a passage in Bk. XXIII:

> First march the heavy Mules, securely slow,
> O'er Hills, o'er Dales, o'er Crags, o'er Rocks, they go:
> Jumping high o'er the Shrubs of the rough Ground,
> Rattle the clatt'ring Cars, and the shockt Axles bound.

> . . .

> Loud sounds the Axe, redoubling Strokes on Strokes;
> On all Sides round the Forest hurles her Oaks
> Headlong. Deep-echoing groan the Thickets brown;
> Then rustling, crackling, crashing, thunder down.

(138–41, 144–7)

As Pope remarks in n. x, "The Numbers in the Original of this whole Passage are admirably adapted to the Images the Verses convey to us. Every Ear must have felt the Propriety of Sound in this Line,

πολλὰ δ' ἄναντά, κάταντα, πάραντά τε, δόχμιά τ' ἦλθον.

That other in its Kind is no less exact,

The same precision appears for Pope in Homer's expression. *"Aristotle* had reason to say, He was the only Poet who had found out *Living Words;* there are in him more daring Figures and Metaphors than in any good Author whatever. An Arrow is *impatient* to be on the Wing, a Weapon *thirsts* to drink the Blood of an Enemy, and the like."[4] And a comparable power, constantly animating individual passages without distracting us from their main point, is at work in the epithets. "We see the motion of *Hector's* Plumes in the Epithet Κορυθαίολος, the Landscape of Mount *Neritus* in that of Εἰνοσίφυλλος, and so of others; which particular Images could not have been insisted upon so long as to express them in a Description (tho' but of a single Line) without diverting the Reader too much from the principal Action or Figure. As a Metaphor is a short Simile, one of these Epithets is a short Description."[5]

In this last statement we see most conspicuously that Pope's Homer criticism points to an interpretation of the *Iliad* in terms of its total significance, a significance created by the range of poetic means which Pope describes. Homer's most precise choice of word, like his most extended conception of character, is part of one coherent structure. This belief about Homer, in turn, governs Pope's interpretation of the whole. "I think it necessary to take notice to the Reader, that nothing is more admirable than the Conduct of *Homer* throughout his whole Poem, in respect to Morality. . . . If the Reader does not observe the Morality of the *Ilias,* he loses half, and the nobler part of its Beauty: He reads it as a common Romance, and mistakes the chief Aim of it, which is to instruct."[6]

I think we can see, in terms of the annotation which I have been discussing, what Pope means by morality or instruction as opposed to romance. He fears that the *Iliad* will be read as remote from the concerns of a society which has superficially so little in common with it. The romance makes no claim to any level of reality; and it uses the device of distance in time, place, or circumstance to protect the individual temporarily from the pressures of his own world. The *Iliad* uses these means too, but in it they serve the very different purpose of enabling us to see

Τάμνον ἐπειγόμενοι, ταὶ δὲ μεγάλα κτυπέουσαι/πίπτον—"
The success with which Pope has captured a sense of rough and irregular progress becomes apparent as soon as one compares a version like the Loeb with its "and ever upward, downward, sideward and aslant they fared."
4. *Pope's Iliad*, I, C3ᵛ.   5. *Ibid.*, I, C4ʳ
6. *Ibid.*, Bk. xxiv, n. xxi. Austin Warren remarks of this passage, "Pope can hardly have put very deep faith in this last: the whole tenor of his Preface and notes contradict, or at any rate interpret, the remark. But it was the received doctrine with critics as reputable as Le Bossu and Madame Dacier, and Pope passes it on to his reader." *Alexander Pope as Critic and Humanist* (Princeton, Princeton University Press, 1929), p. 107. Warren's error here, I think, is that he interprets "instruct" too narrowly. One does not have to be narrowly didactic in order to instruct, as Sidney or Johnson or Coleridge were well aware when they gave their critical support to aspects of the same idea which Pope is advancing.

more clearly certain basic aspects of our own experience, and of the way in which all men feel and act. This is the "forming of virtue by example" which Sidney expounds as the heart of the heroic poem; Pope fears a misreading of the *Iliad* which will put its splendor and inevitable exoticism in the center of interest to the exclusion of the moral tragedy which actually provides the structure of the poem's action as well as the meaning of its characters and ultimately of its imagery.

This tragedy is instruction of the most important sort. It brings us to an increased understanding of the inseparable relation between ethos and action in human life; and with this awareness the *Iliad* fuses a superb consciousness of the universe in which the relentless workings of this relation belong. The persistence of natural and divine worlds stands as a constant foil there to the ephemeral and self-destroying nature of man.[7] The nature of the *Iliad*'s success as a poem—if that success is taken seriously—makes it constantly relevant to our lives.

But success as a poem means in turn precisely those aspects of Pope's criticism which we have just been considering. For one cannot consider the effectiveness of a verse of Homer without asking what it says, one cannot consider his characters without asking what they mean. For Pope the immediate artistic and the final moral aspects of the poem are, when considered carefully, the same thing. One cannot separate the two statements that Homer is supremely important for his poetry, and supremely important for his insight; instead they must be assimilated to one understanding of the *Iliad*.

4

If such is the view of Homer taken by Pope the critic, what demands does that view make on Pope the translator? As we should expect from both his specific analysis and his general attitude toward the tradition, he feels himself "utterly incapable of doing Justice to *Homer*."[8] Within this admission, however, he asserts two major responsibilities: first, "to give his Author entire and unmaim'd" in such over-all aspects of the poem as fable, character, or sentiments, and second, "to afford some Equivalent in our Language for the Graces . . . in the *Greek*" of the diction and versification which are the translator's "proper Province; since these must be his own, but the others he is to take as he finds them."[9]

Pope's desire to present Homer entire does not mean that he hopes to reproduce him in English, for "it is certain no literal Translation can be just to an excellent Original in a superior Language."[1] The emphasis of the poet-translator will be rather on the quality which he can hope to do something about. "That which in my Opinion ought to be the En-

---

7. For a discussion of the *Iliad*'s use of this contrast, see below, chap. ii, pp. 34–9.
8. *Pope's Iliad*, I, F1ᵛ.   9. *Ibid.*, I, E2ʳ⁻ᵛ.   1. *Ibid.*, I, E2ᵛ.

deavour of any one who translates *Homer,* is above all things to keep
alive that Spirit and Fire which makes his chief Character."[2] The image
of fire constantly turns up in Pope's preface when he is writing about
Homer's achievement; it is a guide for the translator because it is a
dominant quality of the original.

In implementing this quality Pope summarizes the ambitions of the
translator:

In particular Places, where the Sense can bear any Doubt, to follow the
strongest and most Poetical, as most agreeing with [Homer's] Character.
To copy him in all the Variations of his Style, and the different Modulations
of his Numbers. To preserve in the more active or descriptive Parts, a
Warmth and Elevation; in the more sedate or narrative, a Plainness and
Solemnity; in the Speeches a Fulness and Perspicuity; in the Sentences a
Shortness and Gravity. Not to neglect even the little Figures and Turns on
the Words, nor sometimes the very Cast of the Periods. Neither to omit or
confound any Rites or Customs of Antiquity.[3]

Significant here, perhaps, is the fact that most of Pope's recommendations
point only to general correspondences. He does not say that the total
effect of Homer is to be reproduced; he does say that Homer's major
shifts of tone are to be perpetuated. The quality which he calls "Plainness"
in his English obviously cannot be a complete equivalent for the quality
often called by the same name in Homer's Greek. But within the whole
poem in either language the reader should be able to say of various passages, "This is plain, this is elevated, this is grave." When Pope remarks
on the correspondence of sound and sense in the Greek *Iliad,* for instance,
he goes on in the most general terms, "Few Readers have the Ear to be
Judges of it, but those who have will see I have endeavour'd at this
Beauty."[4] He does not claim that his readers will respond in the same way
to both English and Greek but merely that the same general kinds of effect
are present in both poems.[5]

Thus he pays homage directly by trying to perpetuate the poetic qualities which Homer introduced into the European tradition. At the same
time, in insisting on these various qualities of the Greek as potential
qualities of the English, in claiming that "there is often a *Light* in An-

2. *Ibid.,* 1, F3r.   3. *Ibid.*   4. *Ibid.,* F1v.
5. At one point in the preface Pope remarks that the translator of Homer should "copy
him in all the Variations of his Style, and the different Modulations of his Numbers"
(F3r). But such a statement must be understood in terms of the specific analysis of
Homer's style which immediately precedes it. There Pope remarks on the necessity of
"supporting the Poetical Style of the Translation" (E2v) and on the fact that many of
Homer's compound epithets "cannot be done literally into *English* without destroying the
Purity of our Language" (E4r). Like his repetitions, they must be manipulated by the
translator with reference both to the context of the original and to the needs of an
English audience (E4v–F1r). Such a recognition of the necessary differences between
Greek and English, however, implies that when Pope talks of "copying" Homer in
English he refers to the need for a flexible and varied English style but not to the possi-
bility of having the same variations which the Greek has.

tiquity, which nothing better preserves than a Version almost literal,"[6] Pope is opposing the various kinds of "rash Paraphrase" by which certain French translators in particular sought to make Homer palatable. He tries to keep away from the extreme of unthinking reverence—"the Ὁμηρομανία of Madam *Dacier* and others,"[7] but he finds even more dangerous for a translator the opposite attitude. La Motte's rhymed reduction of the *Iliad* to twelve books is perhaps the clearest example of what Pope fears from this view of Homer;[8] it shares in heightened form the danger it seeks to oppose, that of losing touch with Homer through one's limited awareness of him. Mme. Dacier risks this when she gives her approval before her understanding, but La Motte is almost certain to misunderstand Homer through his own assumption that modernity in art necessarily implies progress beyond the ancients. Pope sums up his attitude toward both groups of critics when he remarks that the translator "must hope to please but a few, those only who have at once a Taste of Poetry, and competent Learning. For to satisfy such as want either, is not in the Nature of this Undertaking; since a meer Modern Wit can like nothing that is not *Modern,* and a Pedant nothing that is not *Greek.*"[9]

Because this sense of responsibility is bound both to the present and to the past, certain avowed modifications of Homer will be as inevitably present in the translation as will Pope's avoidance of mere modernity. Indeed it is this very respect for Homer on Pope's part that demands certain positive differences from the Greek. "This pure and noble Simplicity [of style] is no where in such Perfection as in the *Scripture* and our Author. . . . This Consideration . . . may methinks induce a Translator . . . to give into several of those general Phrases and Manners of Expression, which have attain'd a Veneration even in our Language from their use in the *Old Testament.*"[1] Pope's culture can provide certain associations which he regards as a legitimate analogue to Homer's style. He makes a positive use of his culture here as we have already seen him use it negatively in restricting certain of Homer's epithets and repetitions. In each case he is trying to express his devotion to the *Iliad* by bringing to it the most stable aspects of his own language.

This insistence on stability makes him suggest that

6. *Ibid.,* E2ᵛ.   7. *Ibid.,* Bk. XVI, n. li.

8. *Ibid.,* I, E2ᵛ, expresses Pope's fear that "rash Paraphrase" is "in danger to lose the Spirit of an Ancient, by deviating into the modern Manners of Expression." For the issue between La Motte and Dacier see H. Rigault, *Histoire de la querelle des anciens et des modernes* (Paris, 1856), Pt. III, chaps. I, II, VII. The important thing to remember is that Pope is not taking sides in a quarrel; in his disapproval of Idomeneus' speech to his dying opponent, for example (Bk. XIII, n. xxxi), he presents La Motte's view of one of the cruxes in the argument with Mme. Dacier. See *L'Iliade, avec un discours sur Homère . . .* (Paris, 1714), p. 80. La Motte is also responsible for the objections mentioned by Pope at the end of Part I of the "Observations on the Shield of Achilles (v, 1448–9); cf. the *Discours,* p. 145. Pope is interested in the controversy between the Ancients and the Moderns only as long as it can tell him something about Homer's poetry.

9. *Pope's Iliad,* I, F3ᵛ.   1. *Ibid.,* I, E3ᵛ.

Perhaps the Mixture of some *Graecisms* and old Words after the manner of *Milton,* if done without too much Affectation, might not have an ill Effect in a Version of this particular Work, which most of any other seems to require a venerable *Antique* Cast. But certainly the use of *modern Terms* of *War* and *Government,* such as *Platoon, Campagne, Junto,* or the like (which some of his Translators have fallen into) cannot be allowable; those only excepted, without which it is impossible to treat the Subjects in any living Language.[2]

It is significant here that Pope is as concerned that the language be living as that it not be ephemerally modern. The English must provide some equivalent for Homer's style but no more in terms of a nonliving language contrived for the occasion than in terms of some contemporary passing fancy.

For Pope neither of these rejected methods would protect the "fire" which he so often insists must be the chief quality of the English *Iliad.* He suggests instead that the translator of Homer "is to study his Author rather from his own Text than from any Commentaries . . . To consider him attentively in Comparison with *Virgil* above all the Ancients, and with *Milton* above all the Moderns."[3] Such a suggestion really demands that the translator fuse his best powers as poet and critic. He must recognize that those powers are indeed inseparable in a good poet working with the tradition—who must learn from Homer if he is to develop the best in himself—and that they are doubly necessary if the poet is going to attempt a realization in his own language of the very poem which has initiated for his culture many of the larger poetic means on which he constantly relies.

As a translator Pope cannot deny his own time and his own language, then, while as a critic and poet he cannot deny that the sources of his strength in English often lie outside of it—in Homer and Virgil as well as in Milton. Somehow he must mediate between what the language available to him is at its richest and all that has enabled it to perfect that richness. Pope the translator, like Pope the critic and poet, is persuaded of the contemporary aliveness of the tradition within which he works and therefore persuaded of his duty toward it. While he knows and states that he cannot reproduce Homer in English, he also insists that he must do the one kind of justice possible—he must attempt in the translation to show Homer in terms of poetic qualities which received their primary impetus from him and in terms of other formal qualities of the living language which may, like a Biblical style, for particular reasons give a vigorous and yet disciplined equivalent to the Greek.

2. *Ibid.,* I, E4ʳ.   3. *Ibid.,* I, F3ʳ⁻ᵛ.

5

This attitude of Pope's toward the translation of Homer includes one important and quite specific problem. How is the poet adequately to supply a "Diction and Versification" for that in the Greek? Pope says that he cannot be merely modern, which implies in terms of Pope's other attitudes that he cannot depend merely upon himself.[4] In addition to the fact that his language belongs to the whole society, then, there should be some positive check on the vagaries of an individual writer while he is dealing with a central aspect of his whole culture such as the *Iliad*. We have already seen that the careful study of Homer is in itself one such check, but as Pope sees it there should also be certain directing forces within or close to the language of the translation.[5]

The Earlier English Translators of Homer

Before Pope, Homer received extensive English development in the versions of Chapman, Ogilby, and Hobbes. For Pope, however, their work is directly useful more as a warning than as an aid. Chapman on the one hand, Ogilby and Hobbes on the other, illustrate two great dangers for the translator.[6] Chapman maintains a rhetoric which too often seems out of control; he is evidently unaware of the fact that Homer seldom wastes words and has almost always a reason for his discursiveness. Ogilby and Hobbes fail through flatness rather than fustian; they make no pretense at any consistent poetic attitude. Pope finds their "meanness" even less satisfactory for an *Iliad* translation than Chapman's misplaced violence.

Pope remarks of Chapman that he writes as "one might imagine *Homer* himself would have writ before he arriv'd to Years of Discretion."[7] He has Homer's "daring fiery Spirit" without his indispensable prudence; his tastes are partial and his patience short.[8] These personal qualities express themselves, furthermore, not only in the language of individual passages but also in what Pope regards as a positive irresponsibility toward Homer's statements. He protests of Chapman, "He appears to have had a strong Affectation of extracting new Meanings out of his

4. Pope's view of the tradition, that is, identifies a knowledge of the past with a knowledge of individual poetic limitations. Knowing Homer and Virgil, one cannot see his own work as he might if he were ignorant; he cannot continue in the arrogance of his isolation.

5. I shall limit myself here to the kind of guidance which Pope describes in his preface and notes. It is clear, however, that this guidance is an active force in the translation itself; see below, chap. ii, secs. iv, v.

6. *The Iliads of Homer Prince of Poets . . . Donne according to the Greeke by Geo: Chapman* (London, 1611); *Homer his Iliads . . . John Ogilby* (London, 1660); *Homer's Iliads . . . Tho. Hobbes* (London, 1676).

7. *Pope's Iliad*, I, F2r.   8. *Ibid.*

Author, insomuch as to promise in his Rhyming Preface, a Poem of the Mysteries he had revealed in *Homer*."⁹

What is the difference for Pope between this development of new meanings in Chapman and those which he indicates as necessary in his own poem? As he says of Chapman, "he has frequent Interpolations of four or six Lines, and I remember one . . . where he has spun twenty Verses out of two."¹ Such a policy of expansion is directed, Pope feels, toward purely personal developments in Chapman's poem; "it is a Liberty he frequently takes, to draw any Passage to some new, far-fetch'd Conceit of his Invention . . . ; he prepares it by several additional Lines purposely to prepossess the Reader of that Meaning."² The speeches of Hector, Paris, and Helen in Book VI seem—as Pope mentions in the same note—egregious examples of augmentation. Hector's criticism of Paris there is prefaced by a twelve-line introduction which explains in detail Chapman's own interpretation of the passage.³

Of course Chapman is "true to his original" in the fact of passion, if not in its form and discipline. There is often life in his poetry; his difficulties for Pope arise from the fact that that life is so eccentric and so extreme in its developments of Homer. But Chapman's constant desire to expound the poem's concealed meaning at least encourages some exploration and development in the English. Neither Ogilby nor Hobbes, on the other hand, has in his language the gift of life at all—except for the unconscious humor in their versions which at any moment, as Pope points out, may create a burlesque of Homer. Hobbes has a particular talent for this; and as a result his translation often sounds a bit like *Hudibras*:

> And there sat *Sleep* in likeness of a Fowl,
> Which Gods do *Chalcis* call, but Men an Owl.⁴

He has other vices in addition to his failure with the poetry; he distorts Homer by frequent and random abbreviations or omissions. "As for its being esteem'd a close Translation," says Pope of his version, "I doubt not many have been led into that Error by the Shortness of it . . . He sometimes omits whole Similes and Sentences."⁵ By his neglect of

9. *Ibid.* Cf. Chapman, *The Iliads of Homer*, A1ᵛ.
1. *Ibid.*   2. *Ibid.*, Bk. v, n. lvii.
3. Chapman, *The Iliads of Homer*, p. 90. Chapman maintains that Hector is bringing the bitterest irony to bear on Paris' effeminacy. Pope in Bk. VI, n. xxxiv suggests that the main artifice of the speech lies in the skill with which Hector finds a more praiseworthy motive for Paris' indolence than that of which he is really guilty. As a result he can correct Paris without enraging him. The central disagreement between Chapman and Pope is not of critical interpretation, however, so much as of procedure with the text. Granted that that text cannot be Homer's, how far is one justified in expanding it by his own speculation?
4. In Bk. XIV, n. xxxiii Pope remarks with considerable restraint, "*Hobbes* has taken very much from the Dignity . . . in translating the present Lines in this Manner."
5. *Pope's Iliad*, I, F2ᵛ. Cf. *The Iliad of Homer . . . done from the French by Mr.*

the similes, indeed, Hobbes destroys Homer for Pope far more effectively than by his mere truncation of narrative. In Book III, for instance,
where the old men on the wall are compared to grasshoppers, we fail to
understand Helen's beauty unless we know through the simile how far
from all passion these sudden admirers are.[6] By sacrificing it Hobbes
betrays Homer in a way which weakens his own poem; we are likely to
feel, along with Pope, that he fails in his duty to the Greek and in his responsibility to the English as well.

But Pope feels that Hobbes also wanders from Homer in other destructive ways. He often mistakes the sense of a passage and at times
adds to it.[7] In one striking case he recognizes—as Chapman fails to do
—the reference of a word in the Greek; but then he adds two lines which
negate the meaning he has just presented.[8] He may at times reproduce
a simile of Homer's and not understand it so that he fails to fit it at all
to the action.[9] And for all his "brevity," he rambles in the presentation
of some comparisons, the mere statement of which would be adequate
to the passage.[1] Hobbes fails for Pope, in short, not merely because he
abbreviates Homer but because he constantly alters him for no discernible
consistent purpose. His freedom is really as extreme as Chapman's,
while it is justified neither by the power to write poetry nor by an informing idea of the poem's total meaning.

The prosy literalness of certain passages is one of several errors in
Hobbes; for Pope it seems to be Ogilby's overpowering defect. His translation is, indeed, a fine example of the impossibility of vigor in a word-
for-word translation—and as such Pope sees it. In a note on the literal
Greek he remarks, "How oddly this would appear in our Language I
appeal to those who have read *Ogilby*."[2] At another point he tells us

---

Ozell (London, 1712), Preface, A7ʳ⁻ᵛ: "As for *Hobbes*'s Translation of *Homer,* which
is so much cry'd up for a faithful though a bald one, I have had the Patience to read the
three first Books . . . I confess he is the closest of any, except Madam *Dacier,* and yet
he is strangely out in some very plain Things."

6. Lines 150–2 of the Greek, 199–202 in Pope. See Pope's n. xx for an analysis of the
pertinence of the simile to the old councilors. Translated baldly the Greek runs: "Because of old age they had now ceased from battle, but they were good speakers, like
cicadas that sit upon a tree in a forest, and pour forth their lily-like voice . . ."

7. *Pope's Iliad,* I, F2ᵛ.

8. *Ibid.,* Bk. v, n. lxvi: "By the *Hours* here are meant the *Seasons;* and so *Hobbes*
translates it, but spoils the Sense by what he adds,

> Tho' to the Seasons *Jove* the Power gave
> Alone to judge of early and of late,

Which is utterly unintelligible, and nothing like *Homer*'s thought."

9. See *Ibid.,* Bk. XIII, n. xxix for one mention of such an error.

1. *Ibid.,* Bk. xv, n. vii indicates one of these excursions.

2. *Ibid.,* Bk. III, n. xxx; Ogilby obscures the purpose of Homer's description.
Though the Greek, as Pope remarks, "means no more than to describe that Behaviour
which is commonly remarkable in a modest and sensible Man who speaks in publick,"
Ogilby gives a wild violence to Ulysses; "you would have thought/Him Fool, or Mad,
or with blind Rage distrought." Cf. a remark on the "servility" of both Ogilby and
Hobbes in Bk. IV, n. vi.

of the latter's faithfulness to numbers in the Catalogue of Ships, but adds, "a Poem contracts a Littleness by insisting on such trivial Niceties."[3] Ogilby seems of course bound to write "mean" verse, since he has no care for the effect of his English. Once in a great while Hobbes stumbles upon a vigorous line, but Ogilby never experiments so far. A deadly faithfulness stays always with him; he destroys the delight of Homer by combining with his own lack of talent as a poet a completely undiscriminating zest for the minutiae of the Greek.

Pope's objections to all three of these versions have common bases, and bases which illuminate still further the goal he set for himself as well as the kind of aid he looked for in achieving it. His criticism has two objects, that which stems from poetic failure and that which stems from a misunderstanding—whether ignorant or willful—of Homer's meaning. Much of the time, furthermore, these two objections combine as Pope considers the work of the three earlier translators. If Chapman, for instance, is to indulge his wholesale desires for phrase making and allegory, he can do so only by modifying Homer drastically; and this he does at the grave risk of writing passages which at their very best will be bad through a failure to fit into the whole poem.

Such limitations are clearly not those which Pope regards as inevitable in any translation; they do not stem from the basic differences between the English and Greek languages and cultures. Most lacking in these translations for Pope, as a result, are the very qualities of continuity and relationship within the heroic tradition with which we have seen him concerned both as a critic and as a theorist of translation. As he sees the earlier translators, their developments of Homer grow from personal concerns; through their manipulation the *Iliad* often loses its central heroic quality.

English Poetry before Pope

Where his interest in the earlier translators must be negative, his interest in earlier writers of the English heroic tradition is highly positive. It is the quality of being in touch with the living past which calls forth his comment not only on Milton but also on Spenser and Dryden.

Pope praises Dryden, not primarily for his fragmentary translations of the *Iliad* but rather for his larger success in solving the very problem in which Pope is seeking guidance: "I would no more have attempted *Homer* after him than *Virgil*, his Version of whom (notwithstanding some human Errors) is the most noble and spirited Translation I know

---

3. *Ibid.*, Bk. II, n. xxxiii; an ungainly number, in calling attention to itself, will stand out beyond far more significant aspects of the Catalogue of Ships. Cf. the last couplet of the third stanza in the 1798 version of *The Thorn*:

> "I've measured it from side to side;
> 'Tis three feet long, and two feet wide."

in any Language."[4] Even from such a general remark we can see that
Pope finds in Dryden's *Aeneid* a way of avoiding the flaccidity of Hobbes,
the meanness of Ogilby. A long poem adequate to his concepts both of
English and of the original already existed; he could depend upon at
least one heroic translation within the larger framework of the tradition.[5]
And as several of his notes show, he was able as a result to do things which
would have been impossible without Dryden.[6]

The help of Milton and Spenser is of a rather different sort. To them
Pope owes above all the prominence of heroic poetry in English literature. If Dryden showed the heroic to be possible in translation, they gave
English form in very different ways and degrees to that "abstract ideal
of the classical epic" which Tillyard points out as having held such interest
for Pope.

As one would expect, Pope finds Spenser realizing this ideal in a rather
"oblique" way, to use Mr. Tillyard's word. But in six or eight notes he
is recognized as an epic poet—as a poet who draws from Homer important lessons for his own guidance and one who is able to develop within
English poetry what he has learned. He has "opened" a great many suggestions in Homer, just as Pope himself often comments on having done.[7]
As a result he has established two things in English—the poetic value of
certain stock heroic means like the catalogue,[8] and the presence within
our idiom of imagery and ways of speaking which, as Pope sees them,
do justice to both Homer and English.

Indeed Pope makes his recognition of this achievement emphatic by
picking as one of his chief examples a passage from *The Faerie Queene*
which seems at first to grow much more from Spenser's interest in pastoral than from his consciousness of epic.

> As gentle Shepherd in sweet Even-tide,
> When ruddy *Phoebus* 'gins to welke in West,
> High on a Hill, his Flock to viewen wide,
> Marks which do bite their hasty Supper best;
> A Cloud of cumb'rous Gnats do him molest,
> All striving to infix their feeble Stings,
> That from their Noyance he no whit can rest,

4. *Ibid.*, I, F2v.

5. Dryden, like Pope, could find help in the development of an English heroic language by translators like Sandys; see below, chap. II, pp. 56–7.

6. See below, chap. II, pp. 60–2.

7. Pope remarks in Bk. XIII, n. lv, "This Simile is very short in the Original, and requires to be open'd a little to discover its full Beauty. . . . I fancy it gave the Hint for
a very fine one in *Spenser,* where he represents the Person of *Contemplation* in the Figure
of a venerable old Man almost consum'd with Study."

8. In his "Observations on the Catalogue," *ibid.*, I, 179, Pope gives his highest praise
to Spenser's use of it. His "Enumeration of the *British* and *Irish Rivers* . . . is one of
the noblest in the World; if we consider his Subject was more confined, and can excuse
his not observing the Order or Course of the Country; but his Variety of Description,
and Fruitfulness of Imagination are no where more admirable than in that Part."

But with his clownish Hand their tender Wings
He brusheth oft, and oft doth mar their Murmurings.

As Pope regards it, this passage "is very much in the Simplicity of the old Father of Poetry."[9] As we see it, furthermore, it is very much in the simplicity of *The Shepherd's Calendar;* its effectiveness is powerful enough to strike us as a parallel to Homer's because the passage rises toward his poetry by its own means. We should be willing to grant with Pope, I think, that through such independence it gives a sense of Homer which a bad direct translation of one of his rural similes cannot convey.

Pope's chief explicit source of guidance with the English of his poem, however, is of course found in *Paradise Lost.* His veneration for Milton is well known,[1] but it is particularly significant to us here as a partial revelation of his attitude toward the continuing presence of Homer and heroic poetry in the English tradition.

Pope directs a good deal of critical attention to the actual use of the *Iliad* by Milton. The latter does constantly what we have seen Pope espouse as a major task of the poet; he thinks through his situation in terms of what has preceded it in poetic achievement, seeking the means to make his own work stronger by his very insistence that it does not stand alone.[2] Such a reciprocal relationship is evident in Pope's remark at one point, "I cannot conclude the Notes on this Story of *Jupiter* and *Juno* without observing with what particular Care *Milton* has imitated the several beautiful Parts of this Episode, introducing them upon different Occasions as the Subjects of his Poem would admit. . . . the very Turn of *Homer*'s Verses is observed, and the Cadence, and almost the Words, finely translated."[3] Certain aspects of Homer receive in this way a new life in English; not only does Homer lend his strength to Milton, but he receives it again renewed through its presence in the work of another poet.

It is this poetic awareness of Homer, present to Pope's eye at so many points in *Paradise Lost,* which suggests to him the general relevance of Milton's work to his own problem of translation. Speaking of Homer's skill in the development of simile he remarks, "The Poet breaks out into this Description with an Air of Enthusiasm, which greatly heightens the Image in general, while it seems to transport him beyond the Limits of an exact Comparison. And this daring manner is particular to our Author above all the Ancients, and to *Milton* above all the Moderns."[4] For

---

9. *Ibid.,* Bk. xvi, n. xxviii.

1. The selection of parallel passages between Pope and Milton in Raymond D. Havens, *The Influence of Milton on English Poetry* (Cambridge, Harvard University Press, 1922), pp. 573 ff., provides a stimulating reminder of the pervasiveness of Pope's homage.

2. Obviously this does not mean that Milton is "imitating" Homer and Virgil in a narrow sense. But when we read of Mulciber's fall or Adam's lustful invitation to Eve, the English is richer and more effective because of what it shares with earlier poems.

3. *Pope's Iliad,* Bk. xiv, n. xxxvii.   4. *Ibid.,* Bk. ii, n. xxxvi.

Pope the two poets share supremely the quality which we have already noticed under the image of fire, "which is so forcible in *Homer,* that no Man of a true Poetical Spirit is Master of himself while he reads him."[5]

Perhaps this similarity of manner justifies for Pope the extensive quotations from *Paradise Lost* in his own notes, but they serve purposes far more important than the mere information they give. Pope is providing in his notes, after all, the proper background for readers of his poem; and when he insists in such detail upon Milton's perpetuation of Homer, he is really also asking his audience to remember Milton when they read his own translation. And as a result he is reminding them that Homer already has a part of his life in work nearly as contemporary for Pope as *The Magic Mountain* is for us.

But indeed Pope's general reading in earlier English poetry makes him think constantly about places where Homer's kind of writing does and does not reside. When he remarks of Denham's *Cooper's Hill* for instance that "The Descriptions of Places, and Images rais'd by the Poet, are still tending to some Hint, or leading into some Reflection, upon moral Life or political Institution" he sees even so slight an achievement as an analogue to *"Homer'*s indirect and oblique manner of introducing moral Sentences and Instructions."[6] Pope's view of the tradition allows him, in sensing the rich variety of Homer, to find aspects of that variety clearly realized in a wide range of English poetry.

For instance, in his discussion of Achilles' passionate speech to Patroclus just before the latter goes fatally forth to battle, Pope calls to his own mind and the reader's the despairing and angry plea of Northumberland that the cosmos destroy man.

> . . . Now let not Nature's Hand
> Keep the wild flood confined!

As Pope sees him, Shakespeare like Homer "intends to paint a Man in Passion; the Wishes and Schemes of such an one are seldom conformable to Reason; and the Manners are preserv'd the better, the less they are represented to be so."[7] In this kind of creative power the poet's skill with language and his perception of the world meet and merge. And Pope, forced to work with a language which cannot be Homer's, may consider as part of his legitimate working material those in his own language who have shown at various points in their poetry some aspect of Homer's achievement in the *Iliad.*

6

Beyond the explicit comment which I have just mentioned, Pope makes coherent the realization of Homer in his own poetic tradition by his constant discussion of the basic quality which underlies all poetry.

5. *Ibid.,* I, B2ʳ.   6. *Ibid.,* Bk. XVI, n. xxxiii.   7. *Ibid.,* Bk. XVI, n. xi.

"HOMER is universally allow'd to have had the greatest Invention of any Writer whatever. . . . Nor is it a Wonder if he has ever been acknowledg'd the greatest of Poets, who most excell'd in That which is the very Foundation of Poetry."[8] And this foundation is ultimately expressible for Pope only in terms again of that image which he uses constantly, in terms of fire which "in *Homer,* and in him only . . . burns every where clearly, and every where irresistibly."[9] Supreme animation seems to be the primary achievement which Pope is pointing to; "the Reader is hurry'd out of himself by the Force of the Poet's Imagination, and turns in one place to a Hearer, in another to a Spectator." [1] While reading the poem, one becomes a part of it. The poet's imagination creates the illusion of a cosmos, a world around the action adequate both to it and to the reader.

Pope's constant use of parallels between poetry and painting as a critical context for his analyses of Homer's action is one of his chief ways of asserting the nature of this illusion. He remarks of Homer's development of a simile in Book v, for example, "He is sure to make a fine Picture in the whole, without drudging on the under Parts; like those free Painters who (one would think) had only made here and there a few very significant Strokes, that give Form and Spirit to all the Piece."[2] The means of the artist bring parts and whole to a clearer relationship than life usually allows.

Painting provides then a useful image for describing the nucleus of inventive power in selection and arrangement; it is equally helpful in describing a full manifestation of that power as we see it in Homer's ability to make us grasp quickly and coherently the nature of some large event.

Here is a Battel describ'd with so much Fire, that the warmest Imagination of an able Painter cannot add a Circumstance to heighten the Surprize or Horror of the Picture. Here is what they call the *Fracas,* or Hurry and Tumult of the Action in the utmost Strength of Colouring, upon the Foreground; and the *Repose* or *Solemnity* at a distance, with great Propriety and Judgement . . . And indeed every thing is so natural and so lively, that the History-Painter would generally have no more to do but to delineate the Forms, and copy the Circumstances just as he finds them described by this great Master.[3]

The comparison with painting—Pope is in part using it here as a metaphor—helps us to see how Homer has built up a sense of the interdependence of the various parts of one complex action. What Pope is pointing to above all is the order growing out of a sequence of events which give at first the effect of chaos.

As a result the chief use of mentioning painting is that Pope can thus

8. *Ibid.,* I, B1ʳ.   9. *Ibid.,* I, B2ᵛ.   1. *Ibid.,* I, B2ʳ.
2. *Ibid.,* Blc. v, n. xiii.   3. *Ibid.,* Bk. VIII, n. xvi.

introduce a new way of looking at actions which appear as a temporal sequence in the *Iliad*. He does not try to deny this temporal structure[4] but suggests that at the same time it produces in the reader of the poem another sort of organization—one concerned with the interrelatedness of parts to form a whole rather than one which works through a mere sequence of parts. This sense of interrelatedness is the final product of successful invention; and when Pope describes a battle or a council of the gods in terms of painting, he is not pointing to a *means* of poetry but rather to a result of the best poetry. The reading of the *Iliad* is first of all an event involving a certain amount of time and by means of which poetic actions appear in sequence. The same is also true of our first acquaintance with a new picture or a new statue. But in all three cases our awareness of the meaning of the work as a whole is finally based on a simultaneous rather than a sequential consciousness of the meaning of its parts. It is the production of this kind of awareness in us by the *Iliad* which allows Pope to say that painters may work directly from it by different means; they may produce a picture which is analogous to the poem in its patterned relationship of parts.

Most significant is the fact that these specific analyses of the working of invention in a poet depend upon precisely the same base as does Pope's general recognition of the value of the tradition. Homer's practice is a great example of the working of the imagination; but it has its place

4. Nor does he deny, of course, the conventional attitude toward the parallel between poetry and painting. One of his recurrent interests in the Homer annotation is the consideration of the picturesque element in Homer's organization of the various parts of his action. There is no reason to assume, however, that this one aspect of the supposed parallel between the arts need be the only one. Pope remarks in his preface, "*Homer* . . . is perpetually applying the Sound to the Sense, and varying it on every new Subject. This is indeed one of the most exquisite Beauties of Poetry, and attainable by very few . . . I am sensible it is what may sometimes happen by Chance, when a Writer is warm, and fully possest of his Image: however it may be reasonably believed they design'd this, in whose Verse it so manifestly appears in a superior degree to all others . . ." (*ibid.,* I, F1ᵛ). We notice above all here that Pope is *not* confusing the media in which the two arts work. A writer may be "possest of his Image," but it expresses itself in the pattern of verbal sound and meaning rather than in some supposed creation of a picture in words. Dryden was using the parallel in the same way when in an epistle to Sir Godfrey Kneller he remarked, after a protest that portrait painting was the only kind in demand,

> Else should we see your noble Pencil trace
> Our Unities of Action, Time, and Place;
> A Whole, compos'd of Parts, and those the best,
> With ev'ry various Character exprest;
> Heroes at large, and at a nearer view;
> Less, and at distance, an Ignobler Crew.
> While all the Figures in one Action joyn,
> As tending to Compleat the main Design.
> (151–8)

R. W. Lee, "*Ut Pictura Poesis:* The Humanistic Theory of Painting," *Art Bulletin, 22* (1940), 197–269, remarks on this Dryden passage but without fully recognizing that Dryden's interest is in the common fact of design rather than in specious similarities of technical procedure. (See p. 259 and n. 302.)

within a still larger structure of successful imaginative work in which both Pope and Homer may stand, if Pope is successful in establishing certain relationships between his translation and the original. These relationships, as we have already seen, depend for Pope upon the belief that a poet does not operate adequately except in a context which by himself he is powerless to create. Just as the rhythm of a line or the development of a character is dependent for its validity upon the total structure within which it exists, so the poet is dependent upon the tradition to which he belongs and which he alters through his successful assimilation to it and of it. All of this is to say that invention or imagination, which at its most immediate works with the relation between sounds and meanings, at its most inclusive works with the relation between poets and hence implicitly between societies and patterns of the world. The order within the *Iliad* is for Pope analogous to the relations of order between the *Iliad* and *Paradise Lost*.

And indeed it is the multiple character of this order which makes the translator's task so precarious a balance between liberty and discipline. For the adequate translator in Pope's terms is a special kind of artist, in a double relation to the tradition by virtue of his duty to another poem as well as his debt to it.

Accepting the fact that his translation cannot be the original, Pope must somehow embody in it his belief that without Homer English poetry would not exist in its present form. He must, in short, attempt to express his necessary differences from Homer in such a way that we are aware of the intimate relationships as well. It is in terms of those relationships that Pope analyzes the structure of the *Iliad,* where Homer's success is defined by means of "permanent" standards of judgment; it is in their terms that he criticizes Chapman and praises Dryden; it is in their terms that he sees his own "original" poetry. If he is to do justice, then, it must be to the essential poetic qualities of Homer as he sees them but also to the fact that those qualities are an inseparable part of the development of poetry between Homer's time and his own. If "nature" and Homer are the same, an *Iliad* translation must pay homage to them both; and nature in this sense is best seen in the highest achievements of the poetic tradition. Homer's place in that tradition and his identification with nature are one; if Pope is to succeed as a translator in his own terms, he must give us some idea through his English poetry of what the identification means. He must present Homer in terms of his own best knowledge of poetic excellence.

II

The Style of a Heroic Poem

I

THE POETIC TASK which we have seen accepted by Pope—
that of making his translation deal in some way with Homer,
with the heroic tradition, and with the broader tradition of
English poetry—will take two chief and familiar forms. Pope will have
to be responsible simultaneously to the local structures and to the complete meaning of his version of the *Iliad*. And while in one way these are
not separate elements of a completed poem, they do demand separate
treatment by the critic. Although made from minute particulars, the
structure of a long poem assumes its own pattern; while on the other
hand each particular has its unique effect as well as its general contribu-
tion.

Both these aspects of a poem are products of invention or imagination
as we discussed them in Chapter I; a main concern of the present chapter
is an exploration of the local or minute aspects of Pope's inventive power.
When we have seen what his style does with the Greek *Iliad,* we shall be
able in Chapter III to form some idea of the relation which the meaning
of his translation as a whole has to its original.

2

Before we consider closely the problems of Pope's style, however,
we should perhaps notice briefly some of the chief qualities of Homer's,
the very qualities which as Pope sees it must inevitably be sacrificed in
translation.[1] Taken as a group Homer's most familiar poetic means are
responsible for the fact that there is present everywhere in his poetry a
persistent world of nature, beyond man and yet always impinging upon
his specific actions—forming, indeed, one important aspect of them.
This is the part of human experience affirmed in the *Iliad* and *Odyssey*
by the great standard repetitions, for instance—Ῥοδοδάκτυλος ἠώς,
οἴνοπα ποντον (rosy-fingered dawn, wine-dark sea), and the like. Their
effectiveness in the poem is paralleled by many compound epithets as
well as other kinds of generalized descriptive word. And all of these
ways of speaking force us to be conscious of the way in which life repeats

1. *Pope's Iliad,* I, E2ʳ, FIᵛ.

itself as it changes, the way in which certain aspects of it are permanent through every kind of action. As C. S. Lewis has said of these expressions,

They emphasize the unchanging human environment. They express a feeling very profound and very frequent in real life . . . The permanence, the indifference, the heart-rending or consoling fact that whether we laugh or weep the world is what it is, always enters into our experience and plays no small part in that pressure of reality which is one of the differences between life and imagined life. But in Homer the pressure is there.[2]

There is, furthermore, a quality of interdependence in the poem, which leads us as we read it to combine any particular physical deed or emotional state with the unending reiterations of the sun's rising or the sight of the sea. And there is also, as a result of the epithets applied to man, a constant emphasis upon the individual limits by which he is bound despite any seeming freedom of action in his life. Phrases like πόδας ὠκύς (swift-footed) or the epithets πολύμητις (many-witted) and κορυθαίολος (with shining helmet) emphasize a certain unalterable, always present quality in each hero. He is distinguished from other men, while by that finiteness and separation his mortality as well as his individuality is established. For a novelist like Proust the problem of understanding a character's identity is foremost; in Homer the style, even in its simplest formulas, directs us to a basic consistency both in individual character and in the working of nature.

The fact that men, like natural events, persist in their fundamental qualities is important for the poem because the two kinds of stability have there a constant relation to one another. This relation is built upon a feeling of recurrent *finiteness* in man and an *exhaustless* recurrence of events in nature, which first of all sets up an antithesis between man and nature.[3] We have a contrast in the poem between the assumption that nature is unlimited in time and the recognition that man's repetition of a quality in the actions of his life is always limited by the sureness of his death.

As a result of their mortality, indeed, men—so various in their actions —are not merely stable with reference to their own individual natures. As a group they have also a certain constant and common bondage to nature—Lewis' "pressure of reality" operates within men as well as around them. Death is the chief sign of this pressure; and the variety of human life in the *Iliad* is brought to a common level by the emphasized

2. C. S. Lewis, *A Preface to Paradise Lost* (Oxford, Oxford University Press, 1943), p. 21.

3. *Pope's Iliad*, Bk. XXI, n. xxvi, is a discussion of one of the most striking of the passages which locate Homeric man in his cosmos. As Pope translates it literally there, " 'Shall I (says *Apollo*) contend with thee for the sake of Man? Man, who is no more than a Leaf of a Tree, now green and flourishing, but soon wither'd away and gone?' " In such a statement we do not think about the death of the tree but about the fact that it will be renewed in life while man will not. See the following note.

unity and immortality of a natural world within which everyone lives
and acts. The stress upon death which appears everywhere in the statement of the poem has thus a rhetorical counterpart in its repetitions and
in certain of its epithets.

For these permit us to realize the place of man in nature, to recognize
that the most basic reality for us is quite precisely that sense of individual
mortality which forces itself upon us through our double knowledge
that we have a stable identity and yet are as transient as the seasons.
Nature is the perpetual return of those seasons, as Glaucus points out
to Diomede in a famous simile.

> Like Leaves on Trees the Race of Man is found,
> Now green in Youth, now with'ring on the Ground,
> Another Race the following Spring supplies,
> They fall successive, and successive rise;
> So Generations in their Course decay,
> So flourish these, when those are past away.
>
> (vi, 181–6)[4]

The simile derives its poignancy from its complex relevance; we are and
yet we so tragically are *not* endowed with the qualities of nature—we
have all its transience but not in and for ourselves its endless possibilities
of renewal.

The stylistic ground swell of the *Iliad* is, then, one which tells man
constantly about his awareness of eternity and as relentlessly reminds him
that he is not eternal. But there is a profound identity between the meaning of the poem's style and the meaning of its main action. The fated
death of Achilles and the grasping for honor which results from it are
emblems of the common fate of all men. A hope of glory is the one human
recompense for an inevitable end; the noble speeches of Sarpedon all
point to this fact. Like Achilles he is half a god, and his death foreshadows
that greater death which lies beyond the action of the *Iliad*. His exalta-
tion of mortal fame is actually a reaffirmation of the passionate desire
which Achilles expresses to Thetis in the first book of the poem. The

---

4.   "οἴη περ φύλλων γενεή, τοίη δὲ καὶ ἀνδρῶν.
       φύλλα τὰ μέν τ' ἄνεμος χαμάδις χέει, ἄλλα δέ θ' ὕλη
       τηλεθόωσα φύει, ἔαρος δ' ἐπιγίγνεται ὥρη·
       ὡς ἀνδρῶν γενεὴ ἢ μὲν φύει ἢ δ' ἀπολήγει."

"As the generations of leaves, so also are those of men. As for the leaves, the wind
scatters some upon the earth; but the forest as it blooms puts forth others when the
season of spring has come. Even so one generation of men springs up, and another
passes away."

(vi, 146–9)

In these notes I shall depend heavily upon A. T. Murray's version of the Greek, in the
Loeb Classical Library edition of the *Iliad;* I have silently altered his most extreme
archaisms and inversions, however, and at some points I have modified his vocabulary in
the interest of simplicity. Since he does not sustain or utilize his style, there seems no
point in perpetuating it.

exhortations of Nestor and Agamemnon, as well as the repinings of Diomede in Book VIII, all magnify honor. Even though life is transient— in part *because* it is so—one may give it the permanence of renown.[5] And the static quality of the chief characters is a way of showing that if a man is to achieve this immortality he must choose one course of action rather than another. Through his choice, of course, he gives up the infinite possibility on which the characters of Hamlet or Prufrock are based; he renounces it in order to wrest something from the finite and actual which will not be merely fleeting. The result for the *Iliad* is, if we consider this one quality apart from the rest of the poem, a simple concept of character. But far more significantly the result is a "placing" of man, a showing of the way in which his glory and his limitations combine.

In building up this meaning for its characters, the *Iliad* uses epithet, repetition, and simile as well as the more expected means of dramatic speech. The force of the repetitions is derived, as we have seen, from the fact that they are always inseparable from some sequence of actions. They can as a result relate those actions directly to the recurrent happenings of nature and by doing so build up a particular evaluation of the universe. The epithets, on the other hand, bring into the poem a previously ordered attitude toward the world. They work in the poem, and they may function as repetitions; but even one use of certain epithets makes a judgment about life as the whole poem sees it. J. W. Mackail remarks on several in his *Lectures on Greek Poetry;* "These are peculiarly Homeric in the richness of . . . their meaning; . . . ἁλιμυρήεντα, εἰνοσίφυλλον, αἰθρηγενέτης, the 'seaward-murmuring river,' the 'foliage-tossing mountain,' the 'crystal-cradled north wind.' Two of them applied to war, 'man-ennobling' and 'mortal-destroying'—βροτολοιγός and κυδιάνειρα—give between them something of the whole moral purpose of the *Iliad*."[6] Such terms are obviously not abstract, while just as obviously they present general rather than unique relationships. The last two, indeed, state directly that duality in human experience which it is really the effect of all the epithets to suggest, while the first three convey it by finding certain consistent emotional qualities in our common experience of the physical world.

As a development, then, of the power of the repetitions to present the pressure of external reality, the epithets show man thrusting his mind back upon the world of nature as well as upon that of human society.[7] *Dawn* is the recurrent world, but *rosy-fingered dawn* is that world valued

---

5. See L. Abercrombie, *The Epic* (London, Martin Secker, 1914), pp. 61–4.
6. J. W. Mackail, *Lectures on Greek Poetry* (London, Longmans, 1910), pp. 66–7.
7. See Bowra, *Tradition and Design,* pp. 81–4; and S. E. Bassett, *The Poetry of Homer* (Berkeley, University of California Press, 1938), pp. 162–4.

and estimated by the human mind. And *mortal-destroying Ares* is a reminder of man in the world, accepting the disasters of his life by the very formula through which he insists on them.

If its epithets help to make the content and attitude of the *Iliad* one, this is done in a more elaborate way by the similes. They share with the epithets a relevance to common human experience. The similarity between image and event is never special or esoteric; it is based upon material known to all men. At the same time, however, the effect of this generally valid relationship is brought to bear upon one specific event. The result is not merely an indication of the relationship between one death and all deaths, or one warrior and all courage; it is also in the poem an indication of the particular value of one man, one action. Paris the stallion or Ajax the stubborn jackass is recognized through the simile as possessing an importance for the poem which grows ultimately from the fact that through the similes they dominate the action at some given point. That Hector is later compared to a stallion does not modify our increased awareness of Paris when the simile is first used.

This particularizing power of the similes means, of course, that they are not in any sense mere decoration to the narrative of the poem.[8] Nor are they, on the other hand, directly pertinent in every detail; as C. M. Bowra says, "They emphasize one thing and one thing only, but the thing emphasized is of first importance to the story. The fierce temper of the Myrmidons is like the fierce temper of wolves at work, the angry Achaeans are like angry wasps waiting for their opportunity to attack."[9] Such similes give us precise understanding of an event but also a special kind of understanding. In the midst of violence we are given a sudden detachment from it, while at the same time we perceive it far more clearly than we should if we were merely embroiled in the detail of the action. The similes are frequent in battle scenes, not merely because these tend to be monotonous but also because they are confused and confusing. The similes call our attention to particular parts of the action and so help to resolve a welter of incident, while at the same time they give to the action as a whole constant points of reference and therefore of stability.

The comparisons upon which the similes depend, furthermore, lead us back again to the interaction between man and nature which we have already noticed in other stylistic elements of the poem. The fire and flood of war, the falling leaves of mortality, the hurtling boulder of heroic force, these and dozens more owe their force to a great richness of meaning. Through them we see into an event as it is defined by a detailed structure out of another context, a structure constantly pointing to the

8. Bassett is, I think, somewhat in error on this point; see *ibid.*, pp. 165–6, and cf. Mackail, *Lectures*, p. 67: ". . . in poetry of a high temperature any enrichment which is mere decoration is out of place . . ."

9. Bowra, *Tradition and Design*, p. 117; at times, as Bowra points out, Homer's similes establish several points of correspondence with the action.

heart rather than the surface of the poem's action. At the same time that other context is a fulfillment of the immediate object or event in the poem and evokes some aspect of the total universe within which that event exists. The felling of a tree can suggest simultaneously the death of a hero in battle and his more general subjection to forces outside his control.

By its way of presenting in all its stylistic means the relationship between individual and general, or transient and persistent, the poem makes us recognize two things: the shifting grasp which mortality exercises upon permanence, and the human need for making one structure out of impermanent man and his abiding universe. That these two realizations support one another is as true within the *Iliad* as it is in our general experience. Lewis' "pressure of reality" is not merely present in the repetitions; the style of the whole poem combines that pressure with one human way of accepting and adapting to it.

As a chief result of this achievement with his style, Homer resolves to one order the presence in the universe of man as an actor and man as a contemplator. The suffering of Hector, the contemplation of that suffering by the reader, and his inclusion within its range, are all simultaneously achieved by a mode of writing which allows us to see while, as Pope says, it never allows us to withdraw.[1] Because we are as subject as its heroes to the poem's interplay of natural and human needs, we are also subject to its action even though not to the consequences of that action. We are enabled to understand Homer's world by participating in it, by experiencing the events we look upon.

3

If, as Pope says, the language and versification of a translation are the independent province of a translator,[2] what form has he himself given to his work? And what relation, if any, exists between that form and Homer's use of the rhetoric of his poem as I have described it? In this and the following sections of the present chapter I shall deal with these questions, considering in several of its aspects the "manner" of Pope's version as it deals with the problems raised by the manner of Homer's original.

We should consider first, perhaps, the qualities which mark the version as being by Pope rather than by Arnold or Chapman or even Dryden. Individual signature seems to be apparent above all in certain patterns of syntax and diction by no means peculiar to Pope but recurring in his work with much more consistency than in Chapman or Cowper. If we look at these patterns from the point of view of their guidance of the

---

1. *Pope's Iliad*, 1, B2ʳ: ". . . the Reader is hurry'd out of himself by the Force of the Poet's Imagination, and turns in one place to a Hearer, in another to a Spectator."
2. *Ibid.*, 1, E2ʳ.

meaning, we find that they fall into several groups, all involving pairs of opposed characteristics. It is impossible in one way to separate the qualities of these various groups from the meanings of the individual words which are organized to create them, but my chief concern at the moment is with their nature and function in the poem once they have been organized from individual words.

Old and New Language

This is a general distinction in Augustan diction, one which Geoffrey Tillotson has considered in a brief but provocative essay. "The poetic diction represents the existing mind, the new words represent the freshness of the response. The poet's value is measured by the quality of the new, and also by the quality of the new art with which he manipulates the old."[3]

Tillotson is discussing pastoral and georgic poetry when he makes his remark, and certainly we find there the most striking examples of language whose effectiveness depends upon its twined excitement and tranquillity. One of the most familiar pastoral passages in the *Iliad*, for instance, the much-discussed night piece which concludes Book VIII, is handled by Pope in such a way that we must give a sympathetic hearing to the expected elements of the passage in order to grasp the "new" point it is making.

> As when the Moon, refulgent Lamp of Night!
> O'er Heav'ns clear Azure sheds her sacred Light,
> When not a Breath disturbs the deep Serene;
> And not a Cloud o'ercasts the solemn Scene;
> Around her Throne the vivid Planets roll,
> And Stars unnumber'd gild the glowing Pole,
> O'er the dark Trees a yellower Verdure shed,
> And tip with Silver ev'ry Mountain's Head;
> Then shine the Vales, the Rocks in Prospect rise,
> A Flood of Glory bursts from all the Skies:
> The conscious Swains, rejoicing in the Sight,
> Eye the blue Vault, and bless the useful Light.
> So many Flames before proud *Ilion* blaze,
> And lighten glimm'ring *Xanthus* with their Rays.
> The long Reflections of the distant Fires
> Gleam on the Walls, and tremble on the Spires.
>
> (VIII, 687–701)[4]

3. Geoffrey Tillotson, *Essays in Criticism and Research* (Cambridge, Cambridge University Press, 1942), p. 71.

4.   ὡς δ' ὅτ' ἐν οὐρανῷ ἄστρα φαεινὴν ἀμφὶ σελήνην
       φαίνετ' ἀριπρεπέα, ὅτε τ' ἔπλετο νήνεμος αἰθήρ·
       ἔκ τ' ἔφανεν πᾶσαι σκοπιαὶ καὶ πρώονες ἄκροι
       καὶ νάπαι· οὐρανόθεν δ' ἄρ' ὑπερράγη ἄσπετος αἰθήρ,
       πάντα δὲ εἴδεται ἄστρα, γέγηθε δέ τε φρένα ποιμήν·

The "old" quality here is apparent in a number of the phrases—"Heav'ns clear Azure," "the solemn Scene," "the dark Trees" have all been seen before. Each of them makes us feel that the events described are typical rather than particular.

At the same time, however, these events are being put at the service of a highly precise and individual attitude toward the scene. Pope is treating the moon as a goddess, and he develops her divinity through her regality. A predictable phrase like "the dark Trees" presents the common world to us, the world which is touched by royalty and becomes splendid. The vivid planets are not merely moving in their accustomed paths but paying homage as they do so. And they pay homage to something more than a standardized moon-goddess; Pope uses a typical nature in the passage as a whole so that we will be free to notice its transformation and animation. The natural world is transfigured; trees turn gold and mountains silver, while vales or rocks take on life and energy. The new quality of the passage as a whole grows from the success with which it directs a group of familiar phrases toward an end for which they have not been used before.

The effect of such a manipulation of vocabulary is to give us two ways of regarding an event. The moon is the one we know, and simultaneously a divinity who makes the world new. But the moon and her re-created world are also a simile; we are not left to consider them merely for themselves, because they carry us on toward an understanding of the Trojan attitude to the war at this point. The watch fires are the real center of the sense of glory and new life which pervades the simile. They represent the hoped-for relief of the city; we are at one of the great moments of Trojan triumph, when the years of defensive war seem turned for a moment into victory.

For the war-weary Trojans this is a change of their natural world so unexpected as to be divine. And of course the sense of divinity in the passage suggests that the gods, hostile so long, have at last become friendly to Troy. At the same time, however, we feel as we read the simile an ambiguity of attitude toward the fires which is totally unperceived by the Trojans. As the flames light up the Trojan army, they are

---

τόσσα μεσηγὺ νεῶν ἠδὲ Ξάνθοιο ῥοάων

Τρώων καιόντων πυρὰ φαίνετο Ἰλιόθι πρό.

As in heaven the stars shine brightly around the moon, when the air is windless, and the mountain peaks and high headlands and glens are visible, and the infinite air breaks open from heaven, and all the stars are seen, and the shepherd rejoices his heart; in such multitudes between the ships and the streams of Xanthus shone the fires that the Trojans kindled before Ilium.

(VIII, 555–61)

In Ogilby's version of Hector's charge to his troops to build the fires (508–9 in the Greek) we get a hint of the hope which Pope builds so high in the night piece:

Whose chearing Fires all Night may gild the Skies
With Splendour, till the joyful Morning rise.

There is nothing of this in Pope's translation of the passage, 632–3.

a presentiment of the future, reminding us of Zeus' prophecies and the inescapable fate of the city. The conventionality of the concluding lines creates the most ironic, because most gentle and seemingly innocent, association of Troy and fire.

This mingling of familiar language with that which has been formed for some precise purpose in the passage really sharpens our attention; we are all the more aware of the unique perception because it is presented as part of something not at all unique. Not only in passages of natural description but in narrative like

> Thus having spoke, th'illustrious Chief of *Troy*
> Stretch'd his fond Arms to clasp the lovely Boy.
> The Babe clung crying to his Nurse's Breast,
> Scar'd at the dazling Helm, and nodding Crest.[5]
>
> (VI, 594–7)

the pattern of standard epithets reflects a world of codified values as grown men and women see them—values set off against the childish fright of Astyanax, who does not realize that fond arms and a nodding crest can go together and knows only that he is "scar'd."[6] The standardized description of Hector allows us to concentrate on this one point rather than move through a distracting variety of observations.

In many passages the relationship of expected and fresh response takes the form almost of a metamorphosis from the first to the second. In a simple fragment of battle description, for instance, like

> Deep in his Breast he plunged the pointed Steel;
> Then, from the yawning Wound with Fury tore
> The Spear, pursu'd by gushing Streams of Gore;
>
> (XII, 478–80)[7]

obvious conventionality is bound up with equally obvious realism. The second, indeed, seems in part to result from the first; the savagery of the event is supported by a swiftness of narrative which the stylized

5.   Ὣς εἰπὼν οὗ παιδὸς ὀρέξατο φαίδιμος Ἕκτωρ.
ἂψ δ' ὁ πάϊς πρὸς κόλπον ἐϋζώνοιο τιθήνης
ἐκλίνθη ἰάχων, πατρὸς φίλου ὄψιν ἀτυχθείς,
ταρβήσας χαλκόν τε ἰδὲ λόφον ἱππιοχαίτην,
δεινὸν ἀπ' ἀκροτάτης κόρυθος νεύοντα νοήσας.

So saying, illustrious Hector stretched out his arms to his boy, but the child shrank back crying to the bosom of his fair girdled nurse, frightened at the look of his dear father and dreading the bronze and crest of horse hair as he perceived it waving dreadfully from the top of the helmet.

(VI, 466–70)

6. Cf. Robert Frost's "They cannot scare me with their empty spaces." The word opens up a childhood world which both Pope and Frost then set against a mature situation.

7.   ἀλλ' ὅ γε Θεστορίδην Ἀλκμάονα δουρὶ τυχήσας
νύξ', ἐκ δ' ἔσπασεν ἔγχος·

He struck with a thrust of his spear Alcmaon, son of Thestor, with sure aim, and drew forth the spear again.

(XII, 394–5)

language greatly furthers. The phrase "gushing Streams of Gore," for example, would seem pat and false considered by itself, but together with the factual violence of "the pointed Steel" or "tore the Spear" it helps to create a valuable sense of suddenness. The man is dead before we quite realize what has happened; and this is so in part because the language allows us to assimilate the whole event so rapidly.

In other, less climactic circumstances such a combination of stylistic means may actually help us to dwell on the texture, the richness of some particular event. When Achilles hospitably receives the Grecian embassy in Book IX, ritual and hunger curiously mingle to govern the entertainment:

> . . . *Patroclus* o'er the blazing Fire
> Heaps in a Brazen Vase three Chines entire:
> The Brazen Vase *Automedon* sustains,
> Which Flesh of Porker, Sheep, and Goat contains:
> *Achilles* at the genial Feast presides,
> The Parts transfixes, and with Skill divides.
>
> (IX, 271–6)[8]

"Brazen Vase" or "sustains" is balanced against the flesh of porker, while in the last line the neatness with which Achilles' action is described emphasizes his position as host and also as dominant figure at the feast.

In general, this kind of ordering in language allows the event to be seen either in some sort of implied context (violent activity as the environment of death) or in enough complexity so that one can regard it simultaneously from a number of different points of view (the feast with Achilles as proof both of his hospitality and his power). The old and new language makes us in certain ways look freshly at a common or universal event, and simultaneously it often makes us look at all of that event, makes us see it not from a new point of view so much as from one which combines several of its aspects.[9] The horror of battle and the pleasure of feasting have this in common as Pope develops them; they are presented not as statement but as something to be understood and interpreted in a multiple way.

8.　　　῝Ως φάτο, Πάτροκλος δὲ φίλῳ ἐπεπείθεθ' ἑταίρῳ.
αὐτὰρ ὅ γε κρεῖον μέγα κάββαλεν ἐν πυρὸς αὐγῇ,
ἐν δ' ἄρα νῶτον ἔθηκ' ὄϊος καὶ πίονος αἰγός,
ἐν δὲ συὸς σιάλοιο ῥάχιν τεθαλυῖαν ἀλοιφῇ.
τῷ δ' ἔχεν Αὐτομέδων, τάμνεν δ' ἄρα δῖος Ἀχιλλεύς.

So he spoke, and Patroclus obeyed his dear comrade. He threw down a great meat tray in the light of the fire, and laid on it a sheep's back, and a fat goat's, and the back of a large hog rich with fat. And Automedon held them for him while noble Achilles carved.

(IX, 205–9)

9. Chaucer's "Knight's Tale" is a strikingly successful fusion of conventionalized and realistic language for ends quite similar to Pope's—the bodying forth of significant and moving action which must be regarded in terms as far as possible from the colloquial and commonplace.

Abstract and Concrete Language

A multiple and yet ordered presentation of the poem's statement is also sustained by the interplay between abstract and concrete views of an incident. This occurs constantly in treatments of detail:

> . . . a Charger yet untouch'd by Flame;
> Four ample Measures held the shining Frame:
> (XXIII, 333–4)[1]

or

> "Lost is *Patroclus* now, that wont to deck
> Their flowing Manes, and sleek their glossy Neck.
> Sad, as they shar'd in human Grief, they stand,
> And trail those graceful Honours on the Sand!"
> (XXIII, 347–50)[2]

But it is also a characteristic way of organizing more complex sections of the poem. Priam calls out to the guards in Book XXI,

> "You to whose Care our City Gates belong,
> Set wide your Portals to the flying Throng.
> For lo! he comes, with unresisted Sway;
> He comes, and Desolation marks his Way!
> But when within the Walls our Troops take Breath,
> Lock fast the brazen Bars, and shut out Death."
> Thus charg'd the rev'rend Monarch: Wide were flung
> The op'ning Folds; The sounding Hinges rung.
> *Phoebus* rush'd forth, the flying Bands to meet,
> Stroock Slaughter back, and cover'd the Retreat.
> (XXI, 622–31)[3]

"Desolation," "Death," and "Slaughter" have transparently special functions in this passage. They seem to be above all ways of manipulating the

---

1.   αὐτὰρ τῷ τριτάτῳ ἄπυρον κατέθηκε λέβητα
      καλόν, τέσσαρα μέτρα κεχανδότα, λευκὸν ἔτ' αὔτως·

. . . for the third he set forth a cauldron untouched by fire, a beautiful one holding four measures, white as at the first.

(XXIII, 267–8)

2.   "τοίου γὰρ κλέος ἐσθλὸν ἀπώλεσαν ἡνιόχοιο,
      ἠπίου, ὅς σφῶϊν μάλα πολλάκις ὑγρὸν ἔλαιον
      χαιτάων κατέχευε, λοέσσας ὕδατι λευκῷ.
      τὸν τώ γ' ἑσταότες πενθείετον, οὔδεϊ δέ σφι
      χαῖται ἐρηρέδαται, τὼ δ' ἔστατον ἀχνυμένῳ κῆρ."

". . . they have lost such a valiant and glorious charioteer, and such a kind one, who would often pour soft oil upon their manes when he had washed them in clear water. For him they stand and mourn, and their manes are trailing on the ground, and the two stand there grieving at heart."

(XXIII, 280–4)

3.   "Πεπταμένας ἐν χερσὶ πύλας ἔχετ', εἰς ὅ κε λαοὶ
      ἔλθωσι προτὶ ἄστυ πεφυζότες· ἦ γὰρ 'Αχιλλεὺς
      ἐγγὺς ὅδε κλονέων· νῦν οἴω λοίγι' ἔσεσθαι.
      αὐτὰρ ἐπεί κ' ἐς τεῖχος ἀναπνεύσωσιν ἀλέντες,

scale of the action, of giving it the greatest possible magnitude while keeping its tone away from mere grandiloquence. As a result of the combination of these terms with this particular event, furthermore, we apply them to Achilles and find that without losing any of their abstractness they are also expressions of his individual power. He is the one mortal in the poem about whom such extremes of statement can be made and have them remain statement. The combination of abstract and concrete, which in a phrase like "graceful Honours" makes us yoke together such different ways of considering a horse's mane, in a passage like the above makes us experience simultaneously both the action and the force of Achilles' rage which governs it.[4] As the Trojans desperately fly from him, furthermore, the balancing against one another of a hideously immediate action and a most abstract interpretation of it helps us to grasp the importance of the event—to grasp, indeed, that it is the real beginning of the poem's climax.

The interaction of abstract and concrete language has also a considerable influence on the pace of many passages. In a simile, for example, like the famous one of the bees in Book II, the interplay between language which we can take for granted because it is familiar generality and language so precise that we pause over it is largely responsible for the swiftness in the passage as a whole.

> As from some Rocky Cleft the Shepherd sees
> Clust'ring in Heaps on Heaps the driving Bees,
> Rolling, and black'ning, Swarms succeeding Swarms,
> With deeper Murmurs and more hoarse Alarms;
> Dusky they spread, a close-embody'd Crowd,
> And o'er the Vale descends the living Cloud.
>
> (II, 111–16)[5]

αὗτις ἐπανθέμεναι σανίδας πυκινῶς ἀραρυίας·
δείδια γὰρ μὴ οὖλος ἀνὴρ ἐς τεῖχος ἅληται."
"Ὣς ἔφαθ', οἱ δ' ἄνεσάν τε πύλας καὶ ἀπῶσαν ὀχῆας·
αἱ δὲ πετασθεῖσαι τεῦξαν φάος.

"Hold the gates wide open with your hands until the people come to the city in their flight, for in truth Achilles is here at hand as he drives them in rout; now there will be destruction, I think. But when they have found respite, crowded within the wall, then close again the well-fitting double doors; for I fear lest that murderous man leap within the wall." So he spoke, and they undid the gates and thrust back the bars; and the gates being flung wide wrought deliverance.

(XXI, 531–8)

4. When in the preface to *The Age of Anxiety* Auden speaks of "armies with their embossed debates" he is using precisely the same poetic means. In part the method is one of shock; the divergence between physical and intellectual encounter is first suggested by the two words and then reconciled as we consider by means of them the complex relationships of war.

5.   ἠΰτε ἔθνεα εἶσι μελισσάων ἀδινάων,
πέτρης ἐκ γλαφυρῆς αἰεὶ νέον ἐρχομενάων·
βοτρυδὸν δὲ πέτονται ἐπ' ἄνθεσιν εἰαρινοῖσιν·
αἱ μέν τ' ἔνθα ἅλις πεποτήαται, αἱ δέ τε ἔνθα·

As the tribes of swarming bees go forth from some hollow rock, constantly coming

The descriptive adjectives and participles here are for the most part commonplace ones. Removed from this passage, phrases like "deeper Murmurs" or "close-embodied Crowd" are completely standard and everyday. It is their use here together with the one precisely naturalistic word "driving" and the one highly accurate metaphor of the "living Cloud" which makes them effective. The descriptive sufficiency of "rocky Cleft" is apparent in the context of such phrases where it would be worth no comment taken merely by itself; "close-embodied Crowd" assumes a physical significance for bees swarming which it does not have for normal groups of people. And because the relationship of parts is so effective each prepares us for the other, while both aspects of the style steer us to the real point of the passage in its context—its suggestion of the way in which a group of men will become possessed of an idea which makes them act in violent, uncontrollable unanimity and cohesion. Because of their simple character the lines put their main emphasis on this one point, and the mind's assimilation of it can be rapid, while at the same time the variation of quality in the parts, between the concreteness of the second and third lines, the abstractness of the fourth and fifth, keeps the passage as a whole from dullness.

A further striking quality of the phrase "living Cloud" is that considered separately it sounds rather like false rhetoric; its justification, like that of the commonplace generalities, arises from the completed whole in which it participates. But this serves to remind us, of course, of something which it is all too easy to forget. The supposed master of a whole kind of poetic diction, Pope creates his most recurrent characteristic effects by the arrangement of his language; like Yeats he gives us the feeling that these are all words we would have thought of using but that the relationships between them give the poetry a life which we could never claim to have sensed in its component words before.

Metaphorical and Literal Language

It is obvious in the passage I have just discussed, as in several of those earlier in this section, how much Pope owes to his power over metaphor. In the *Iliad,* however, as in the whole body of his "original" work, it is the half-concealed image which is of particular use to him. Pope is perhaps interested in this form of metaphor because his poetry has characteristically another kind of superficial sustaining structure. Conversation, philosophical or moral argument, satiric action, these provide an obvious organization behind which his metaphors are to work. And so in the *Iliad* the narrative structure carries the reader along, but he is free if he wishes to notice that by metaphor, as well as by the other

---

on afresh, and in clusters over the flowers of spring fly in throngs, some here, some there.

(II, 87–90)

means I have described, something is being done through the narrative
and beyond it. In passages like the description of Ulysses:

"But, when he speaks, what Elocution flows!
Soft as the Fleeces of descending Snows
The copious Accents fall, with easy Art;
Melting they fall, and sink into the Heart!"

(III, 283–6)[6]

or the trapping of Nestor:

Nestor alone amidst the Storm remained. . . .
When dreadful *Hector,* thund'ring thro' the War,
Pour'd to the Tumult on his whirling Car.

(VIII, 102, 111–12)[7]

or the anatomy of battle itself:

As when sharp *Boreas* blows abroad, and brings
The dreary Winter on his frozen Wings;
Beneath the low-hung Clouds the Sheets of Snow
Descend, and whiten all the Fields below.
So fast the Darts on either Army pour,
So down the Rampires rolls the rocky Show'r;
Heavy, and thick, resound the batter'd Shields,
And the deaf Eccho rattles round the Fields.

(XII, 175–82)[8]

6.   "ἀλλ' ὅτε δὴ ὄπα τε μεγάλην ἐκ στήθεος εἵη
καὶ ἔπεα νιφάδεσσιν ἐοικότα χειμερίῃσιν,
οὐκ ἂν ἔπειτ' 'Οδυσῆΐ γ' ἐρίσσειε βροτὸς ἄλλος·
οὐ τότε γ' ὦδ' 'Οδυσῆος ἀγασσάμεθ' εἶδs ἰδόντες."

"But when he uttered his great voice from his chest, and words like snowflakes on
a winter's day, then could no mortal man beside compete with Odysseus; then did we
not wonder so to see Odysseus' aspect."

(III, 221–4)

7.   Νέστωρ οἶος ἔμιμνε Γερήνιος, οὖρος 'Αχαιῶν,

• • •

. . . τόφρ' "Εκτορος ὠκέες ἵπποι
ἤλθον ἀν' ἰωχμὸν θρασὺν ἡνίοχον φορέοντες
"Εκτορα.

Only Nestor of Gerenia remained, the warder of the Achaeans . . . meanwhile the
swift horses of Hector came on through the tumult bearing a bold charioteer, Hector.

(VIII, 80, 88–90)

8.   . . . νιφάδες δ' ὡς πῖπτον ἔραζε,
ἅs τ' ἄνεμος ζαής, νέφεα σκιόεντα δονήσας,
ταρφειὰς κατέχευεν ἐπὶ χθονὶ πουλυβοτείρῃ·
ὡς τῶν ἐκ χειρῶν βέλεα ῥέον, ἠμὲν 'Αχαιῶν
ἠδὲ καὶ ἐκ Τρώων· κόρυθες δ' ἀμφ' αὖον ἀΰτευν
βαλλόμεναι μυλάκεσσι καὶ ἀσπίδες ὀμφαλόεσσαι.

And like snowflakes the stones fell ever to the ground, like flakes that a blustering
wind, as it drives the shadowy clouds, sheds thick and fast upon the bounteous
earth; even so flowed the missiles from the hands of these, of Achaeans alike and
Trojans; and helmets rang harshly, and bossed shields, as they were struck with
great stones.

(XII, 156–61)

an image which may be explicit at one point remains as an important implication of the rest of the passage. A rhyme like "pour-Show'r" is obviously ambivalent in its meaning, but "rolls" and indeed almost all the sounds at the end of the third passage are equally aspects of storm and of battle.

One great value of this kind of extended metaphor is its adaptability to a long poem. The image becomes inseparable from the onward movement of the poem and indeed furthers that movement by providing an order which illuminates the poem's narrative statement. The last line of the description of Ulysses, for instance, would be satisfactory enough if it stood alone; as the development of a metaphor already introduced, however, it climaxes our sense of an irresistible, natural force as the chief attribute of Ulysses' speech.

In all three cases, the conclusion of the image is the most striking part of it; and this is so because there Pope has used common phrases, phrases which have been used so much that we tend to forget they are implicit metaphor. By making them part of an image which, when it is first introduced, does not seem common, Pope restores their original quality again while he alters none of their currency. "Thund'ring" loses its triteness but keeps its ease; the effect is similar to that which we have noticed in other aspects of Pope's rhetoric, where the chief purpose of his organization of language seems to be a combination of ease and excitement. He takes words which we thought we had mastered and shows us how much there is still to be understood both about and by means of them. As a result a passage which starts out to be a simile about battle winds up by being a mutual animation of the war and its image so that at the end we are equally aware of the destructive savagery of nature and the "elemental" character of mass human destructiveness. The image has served the poem by making the reader actually see into the meaning of its narrative further than he otherwise would have.

Clearly none of these poetic means is the unique possession of Pope. They are distinguishing features of his work, however, because he uses them so persistently and because he intertwines them so constantly. Both these things he does cogently and economically because of the organizing power of the couplet. One cannot say that the abstract idea of the couplet comes first and then the rhetorical means of exploiting it; the two aspects of syntax and verse form are not separable in the finished poetry, since each is so superbly adapted to the formal demands of the other. At least in the Homer, however, this adaptation is successful for reasons rather different from those usually given as an explanation for Pope's couplet.

The *Iliad* is Pope's only nonsatiric narrative of any length; in it he has the problem of keeping his reader moving, of asking him to notice what the syntax and verse form are doing without lingering over them so long that he loses his headway in the poem. In *The Rape of the Lock* it is perfectly safe to force a pause over an antithesis:

> Bright as the Sun, her Eyes the Gazers strike
> And, like the Sun, they shine on all alike.
>   (II, 13–14)

But such a double take in the *Iliad* would demand too much at one point. Pope avoids it by combining rather than opposing the poem's various rhetorical elements. When the goddess of dullness says,

> "All my Commands are easy, short, and full:
> My Sons! be proud, be selfish, and be dull."
>   (*Dunciad,* IV, 581–2)

the second series and the first are ironically opposed to one another, the concrete commands of the second not what the abstract statement of the first had led us to expect. But when we see on a battlefield

> Steeds cased in Mail, and Chiefs in Armour bright,
> The gleamy Champain glows with brazen Light.
>   (*Iliad,* XX, 190–1)

the collective character of the second line fulfills and dignifies the factual statement of the first. Without becoming merely abstract, a fact about the battlefield is opened out into a condition of war. And the same distinction holds in the formal structure of the couplets. In the one from the *Dunciad* the parallel construction emphasizes the obvious antithesis of meaning; and the rhyme words are the climax of the antithesis because they are the climax of the seeming parallel of statement, or the parallel as the goddess sees it. For her the full achievement is dullness. In the *Iliad* couplet the rhyme is a true parallel, just as the whole second line is a restatement of one aspect of the first, a raising to the general condition "Light" of the factual "Armour bright." The orientation of the couplet is not merely or even primarily internal; it makes a statement, the chief relevance of which lies in the larger description of battle.

It is above all important to remember, as Arnold and many less competent critics have forgotten, that an enormous number of different things can be done with the couplet form as with Pope's other stylistic means. This is not to deny for a minute that the *Iliad* "sounds like Pope"; my aim in the last few pages has been to show that it does but to show also that Pope can turn his characteristic verse to a great number of different uses. The real basis on which to judge this style, it seems to me, lies beyond the fact that it is among other things obviously Pope's work; we must go on to ask what relation the poem's rhetoric has to the "heroic" kind of writing, and also what relation it has to the Greek *Iliad*. And we must inquire into these relations, finally, as they combine with Pope's own characteristic style to produce the complete translation.

4

Aristotle's remark that the characters of tragedy are "better" than those in our world of today is equally true, of course, for heroic poetry. As Lewis has put it, "Epic, from the beginning, is *solempne*. You are to expect pomp. You are to 'assist,' as the French say, at a great festal action."[9] But this expectation puts very special demands on the nondramatic writer who must pitch his work in the same tone as tragedy but without the means of tragedy. He must show the differences between that better world and our own, but simultaneously he must show its relevance to ourselves. We must feel that the heroic life is not our life and yet that it belongs to our life.

To accomplish this the epic poet must work with the ordering of his action and the ordering of his language. He cannot set his context before a word is spoken as the playwright can. Among the most striking qualities of Homer for Pope, as we noticed in the first chapter is his dramatic power: "The Reader is hurry'd out of himself by the Force of the Action." But this vigor must create its illusion of urgency at two removes; Homer has first to persuade us that we are the spectators of an action before he can convince us that we are participants in it. He must hold us within the world of his poem. We must feel while we are reading that it is the "real" world.

This demand on the artist partially explains why the language of heroic writing is shared among poets more explicitly than that of any other mode. Johnson's well-known remark, that "Pope searched the pages of Dryden for happy combinations of heroick diction, but it will not be denied that he added much to what he found,"[1] is, if we add the names of a dozen other poets, as true in its first part as in its second. These "happy combinations" turn up in translators as obscure for us as Manwaring or Dacier; and they are as obviously a part of the means of Milton or Shakespeare.

Manwaring, for example, who translated a part of Book I of the *Iliad*, included in his version of Chryses' prayer several phrases of the same general sort as those used by Dryden and Pope.

> "O Source of Sacred Light, attend my Pray'r,
> God with the Silver Bow, and Golden Hair;
> Whom *Chrysa, Cilla, Tenedos* obeys,
> And whose broad Eye their happy Soil surveys:
> If, *Smintheus*, I have pour'd before thy Shrine
> The Blood of Oxen, Goats, and ruddy Wine,
> And Larded Thighs on loaded Altars laid,

9. Lewis, *A Preface to Paradise Lost*, p. 16.
1. Johnson, *Lives of the Poets*, III, 238.

Hear, and my just Revenge propitious aid.
Pierce the proud *Greeks,* and with thy Shafts attest
How much thy Pow'r is injur'd in thy Priest."
(Dryden, 1, 57–66)

"Propitious *Phoebus!* Hear thy Suppliant's Pray'rs,
Thou Guardian King, whom chosen *Chrysa* fears;
For whose Protection sacred *Cilla* prays,
Thou glorious Light! whom *Tenedos* obeys;
If e'er thy Priest a grateful Service paid,
Or Bulls and Goats on flaming Altars laid;
O *Smintheus* hear! and with thy Silver Bow
Dart the proud *Grecians,* and revenge my Woe."
(Manwaring, 47–54)

"O *Smintheus!* sprung from fair *Latona*'s Line,
Thou Guardian Pow'r of *Cilla* the divine,
Thou Source of Light! whom *Tenedos* adores,
And whose bright Presence gilds thy *Chrysa*'s Shores;
If e'er with Wreaths I hung thy sacred Fane,
Or fed the Flames with Fat of Oxen slain,
God of the Silver Bow! thy Shafts employ,
Avenge thy Servant, and the *Greeks* destroy."
(Pope, 1, 53–60)[2]

Their share in the Greek accounts for certain similarities between the three passages, of course; but the phrases dealing with Apollo as a god of light are in all three versions added to a literal translation of the Greek. Added also is a tone of religious and social dignity which, except for Dryden's few deviations toward colloquial statement, the three passages maintain.

Indeed these lapses from dignity on Dryden's part are as suggestive of the difficulties of a "high style" as are the frigid proprieties of Manwaring's passage. Dryden provides one kind of propriety, of course, by his use of a rather obviously poetical syntax and alliteration. But this gets out of control in one way just as his oscillation of tone between two of the poeticized phrases—"source of sacred light" and "larded thighs on loaded altars"—does in another. Both kinds of faulty discipline interfere

---

2.   "Κλῦθί μευ, ἀργυρότοξ', ὃς Χρύσην ἀμφιβέβηκας
Κίλλαν τε ζαθέην Τενέδοιό τε ἶφι ἀνάσσεις,
Σμινθεῦ, εἴ ποτέ τοι χαρίεντ' ἐπὶ νηὸν ἔρεψα,
ἢ εἰ δή ποτέ τοι κατὰ πίονα μηρί' ἔκηα
ταύρων ἠδ' αἰγῶν, τόδε μοι κρήηνον ἐέλδωρ·
τίσειαν Δαναοὶ ἐμὰ δάκρυα σοῖσι βέλεσσιν."

"Hear me, thou of the silver bow, who dost stand over Chryse and holy Cilla, and dost rule with might over Tenedos, thou Sminthian, if ever I roofed over a shrine to thy pleasing, or if ever I burned to thee fat thigh-pieces of bulls or goats, fulfil thou this prayer for me: let the Danaans pay for my tears by thy shafts."
(1, 37–42)

with the onward movement of the passage, and the second interrupts in another serious way as well. It presents us with suddenly crude ways of interpreting sacrifice and therefore the gods of the poem. This crudity reaches its high-Dutch climax at the end of Book I:

> "The Reconciler Bowl, went round the Board,
> Which empty'd, the rude Skinker still restor'd.
> Loud Fits of Laughter seiz'd the Guests, to see
> The limping God so deft at his new Ministry.
> The Feast continu'd till declining, Light:
> They drank, they laugh'd, they lov'd, and then 'twas Night."
>
> (I, 802–7)

The life in such a passage is undeniable, but we are forced to ask whether it is not a kind of vitality which interferes with our acceptance of Homer as the master of heroic writing.

In making such a statement one must admit the possibility that there can be different kinds of heroic poetry at different times; but it is certainly fallacious to think that this difference is broad enough to include burlesque.[3] This does not mean, however, as many Milton imitators fancied, that one can seize upon a rather dull high seriousness in language and call it poetic dignity. That is precisely the fault with Manwaring's version of the prayer. His passage seems to have nothing but a manner; it lacks poetic excitement, the quality of fire which Pope constantly calls to our attention in Homer. Manwaring suggests by his language that the heroic world is one of dignity but not that it is one of vital relevance to our nonheroic world.

This sense of relevance Pope provides by two chief means. The first is his relative syntactic naturalness. His vocabulary implies that something out of the ordinary is taking place, but the order of his words implies that the extraordinary event has its relationship to our world. The passage is in the pattern of declarative colloquial speech, though not in the manner of it. The division of parts is sharp, and the sequence of clauses is never broken by parenthetical comment. Pope's second means of giving the passage excitement is his development of the deity of Apollo. Not only does he, like the others, introduce a phrase identifying Apollo with light, but he extends it in the next line with his "bright Presence." In doing so he makes explicit the religious maturity implied by both him and Dryden in calling Apollo the source of light rather than the mere light itself. In opposition to Manwaring's interpretation of him, the god of Pope's passage stands behind and beyond the objects which symbolize him. He is a true deity and not a mere personification of the sun.

The most important thing to remember about such passages is that the shared heroic tone is neither automatic nor easy in its working. One

---

3. Dryden himself makes this point clear, of course, in his *Aeneid* translation, where he succeeds in maintaining the tone of dignity together with a proper liveliness. See chap. ii, pp. 60–2.

is constantly being tempted to violate it for local excitement as Dryden does, or to succumb totally to its conventional aspects as Manwaring does. The means of elevating his poetry, in particular, are present for Pope in the work of many of his predecessors; as we shall see, they can help him in a variety of ways to sustain the world of heroic action. But this help from beyond the poem is only valuable if it is absorbed fully enough so that it becomes effective within the poem. We must consider the chief attributes of an English heroic style both as they come to Pope and as they work for him.

There are perhaps three main aspects of this style. They grow from one another, and they are all directed toward the creation of an attitude which may interpenetrate with the poem's action to keep the reader always convinced that he is in touch with a world of supreme importance. They are by no means peculiar to heroic writing—indeed we have seen certain of them already as aspects of Pope's individual style—but they are of particular value in the developing and sustaining of narrative at its highest pitch.

Immediate Precision and General Significance

The writer of heroic poetry has a double problem of strategy in dealing with his reader. He must not be dull in his immediate effects, but at the same time he must be delightful in such ways that his audience will never forget that the individual stimulating passage is part of something much larger. When Milton describes the creation in Book VII of *Paradise Lost,* for example, he does a remarkable job of conveying the claim which the physical universe makes on our admiration:

> . . . Shoals
> Of Fish that with thir Fins and shining Scales
> Glide under the green Wave, in Sculls that oft
> Bank the mid Sea: part single or with mate
> Graze the Seaweed thir pasture, and through Groves
> Of Coral stray, or sporting with quick glance
> Show to the Sun thir wav'd Coats dropt with Gold,
> Or in thir Pearly shells at ease, attend
> Moist nutriment, or under Rocks thir food
> In jointed Armor watch . . .
>
> (VII, 400–9)

The imagery drawn from human activity works with the highly selective adjectives of the passage to create the independent splendor of the marine world—to make us realize that it *is* a world of its own. Its texture and its action are both evoked as something splendid; ease and beauty combine, not only for the passive creatures but also for the sportive and leisured ones who stray through groves of coral.

At the same time, however, this treatment of a special world is handled in such a way that we gain an increased insight into the larger importance of the whole created universe. Its parts are not merely splendid in themselves but splendid in their relationship to one another. The pastoral world of man helps the passage to develop a sea world, but at the same time the sea world brings us back to man. We come to perceive the wonder of marine order, while we perceive it in terms which also evoke the splendor and beauty of a certain patterned way of regarding human life. Through its new use we suddenly recognize the pastoral for what it is at its best, a way of dignifying and shaping our direct experience of nature without losing the validity of the natural world. Because the beauty of marine life is presented in pastoral terms, the more general meanings of the pastoral tradition come to new life in the poem and direct us toward Adam and Eve.

But this enrichment of our world is even more pervasively the result of the choice of an adjective which is superbly adapted to the individual creature being described, while simultaneously it relates that creature to a world of more universal substances and forms. Just as the pastoral language calls up an immutable world, so language like "green wave," "waved coat," "pearly shell," "jointed armor" creates one in which the permanent qualities of things fuse with their particular appearances. This interaction of immediate and general reaches a climax in *Paradise Lost* with the speech of Raphael to Adam, where style and statement are both concerned with the relationship.

> "O Adam, one almighty is, from whom
> All things proceed, and up to him return,
>
> .   .   .
>
> Each in thir several active Spheres assign'd,
> Till body up to spirit work, in bounds
> Proportioned to each Kind. So from the root
> Springs lighter the green stalk, from thence the leaves
> More aery, last the bright consummate flow'r
> Spirit odorous breathes . . ."
>
> (v, 469–70, 477–82)

For the relation of immediate to general is really a relation of parts to whole; its "jointed armor" sets the lobster within an order, just as the "consummate flow'r" implies that order. In this kind of writing the adjectives are a means of establishing the quality of an immediate object or event in terms of its most significant, its largest context.

This use of language is of course not the possession of a period but of a kind of poetry. It is strikingly evident in Chaucer's style when he is dealing with the chivalric world, and it is one of Tennyson's chief characteristics in the *Idylls of the King*.[4] In Spenser and Shakespeare, further-

---

4. In *The Passing of Arthur,* for instance, Tennyson builds the basic nature of the last battle into his description:

more, we not only see similar ends served but served in ways which share a great deal with Milton and Pope. The precision of Ceres' speech in the Act IV masque of *The Tempest*, for instance, makes a carefully generalized way of writing imply both the importance of fertility for an earth goddess and something of its joy:

> "Hail, many-colour'd messenger, that ne'er
> Dost disobey the wife of Jupiter;
> Who with thy saffron wings upon my flowers
> Diffusest honey-drops, refreshing showers;
> And with each end of thy blue bow dost crown
> My bosky acres and my unshrubbed down,"
>
> (IV, i, 76–81)

Nature here is neither naturalistic nor sentimental; it is instead the subject of a pattern of conventionalized language which fuses for purposes beyond them all certain mythic, factual, and metaphorical possibilities in nature. The honorific adjectives, the discipline of the couplet, the use of verbs which point toward formal events are all qualities familiar in the Augustans and used here for purposes similar, at least, to Pope's in his *Iliad* language. Indeed the compact and seemingly simple way in which the Shakespeare passage enables us to realize both the dignity and the allure of Ceres is a very precise analogy to the *Iliad*'s combining by means of the diction a large action and a precise detail.

This same organizing and fusing power of the diction is for Spenser a way of expressing Prince Arthur's devotion to the love which escapes him and yet which he cannot escape.

> "When I awoke, and found her place devoyd,
> And nought but pressed gras where she had lyen,
> I sorrowed all so much as earst I joyd,
> And washed all her place with watry eyen.
> From that day forth I lov'd that face divyne;
> From that day forth I cast in carefull mynd,
> To seek her out with labor, and long tyne,
> And never vow to rest till her I find,
> Nyne monethes I seek in vain yet ni'll that vow unbind."
>
> (*The Faerie Queene*, I, IX, xv)

> So all day long the noise of battle roll'd
> Among the mountains by the winter sea;
> Until King Arthur's Table, man by man,
> Had fall'n in Lyonnesse about their lord,
> King Arthur. Then, because his wound was deep,
> The bold Sir Bedivere uplifted him,
> And bore him to a chapel nigh the field,
> A broken chancel with a broken cross,
> That stood on a dark strait of barren land.

The chapel which might have been a mere decoration to the action becomes through the diction of the last lines a commentary instead, a reminder of the complete ruin implied by the last battle.

About each part of Arthur's experience we learn only so much as will help us to understand its power over him. Words like "devoyd" or "watry" take on a very specific pathos; they are not mere casual counters because their usual standardized meaning is so completely and personally applicable at this point. And yet at the same time, they work with equally particular uses of words like "divyne" and "carefull" to relate this single event to the general experience of devoted love.[5]

Pope finds ready to his hand, then, not only an acceptance by the poetic tradition behind him of the valid purposes of a generalized diction but also a surprising amount of careful and disciplined use of this language. As a result, when he describes Agamemnon,

> He rose, and first he cast his Mantle round,
> Next on his Feet the shining Sandals bound;
> A Lion's yellow Spoils his Back conceal'd,
> His warlike Hand a pointed Javelin held.
>
> (x, 27–30)[6]

or the shield of Achilles,

> Next, ripe in yellow Gold, a Vineyard shines,
> Bent with the pond'rous Harvest of its Vines;
> A deaper Dye the dangling Clusters show,
> And curl'd on silver Props, in order glow:
> A darker Metal mixt, intrench'd the Place;
> And Pales of glitt'ring Tin th'Enclosure grace.
>
> (xviii, 651–6)[7]

5. In his translation of the *Metamorphoses*, for instance, even a minor poet like Sandys could show the vigor of this mode of writing:

> Forth-with upsprung the quick and waightlesse Fire,
> Whose Flames unto the highest Arch aspire.
>
> (London, 1626, p 2)

> Swift feet no more
> Availe the Hart; nor wounding tusks the Bore.
> The wandring Birds, hid Earth long sought in vaine,
> With weary wings descend into the Mayne.
>
> (p. 8)

> I long to walke among
> The loftie starres: dull earth despis'd, I long
> To back the clouds; to sit on *Atlas* crowne:
> And from that hight on erring men look downe.
>
> (p. 308)

6. ὀρθωθεὶς δ' ἔνδυνε περὶ στήθεσσι χιτῶνα,
    ποσσὶ δ' ὑπὸ λιπαροῖσιν ἐδήσατο καλὰ πέδιλα,
    ἀμφὶ δ' ἔπειτα δαφοινὸν ἑέσσατο δέρμα λέοντος,
    αἴθωνος μεγάλοιο ποδηνεκές, εἵλετο δ' ἔγχος.

So he sat up and put on his tunic about his breast, and beneath his shining feet bound his fair sandals, and afterwards dressed himself in the tawny skin of a lion, fiery and great, a skin that reached his feet; and he grasped his spear.

(x, 21–4)

7.   Ἐν δὲ τίθει σταφυλῇσι μέγα βρίθουσαν ἀλωὴν
        καλὴν χρυσείην· μέλανες δ' ἀνὰ βότρυες ἦσαν,

or the response of Menelaus to Antilochus' apology,

> Joy swells his Soul, as when the vernal Grain
> Lifts the green Ear above the springing Plain,
> The Fields their Vegetable Life renew,
> And laugh and glitter with the Morning Dew:
> Such Joy the *Spartan's* shining Face o'erspread,
> And lifted his gay Heart, while thus he said.
> (XXIII, 678–83)[8]

Pope is being traditional in a way which he himself had already defined. He is making past and present in the language serve one another, and in particular he is making the present serve the past by serving its own precise purposes in a specific passage.

The excitement of specific usage is possible in part, of course, because of the way in which this kind of descriptive word has been used before; but the word is a mere insult to past use if it is not effective in itself. The stability given to the reader by the feeling that he is reading the right language for this kind of poetry must be balanced by a feeling that he is reading the right language for the individual passage. The opulent harvest must be an aspect of the shield as well as of the world it protects; the joy of spring must be, through words like "swells," "Lifts," "springing," equally a joy in the mind.

If the generalization is truly valid for the individual passage, furthermore, a purpose in the poem beyond those which I have already mentioned is also served by it. I suggested in connection with Pope's individual style that the fusion of particular and general contributes to the rapidity of the poem. This sense that one does not have to stop short over a passage combines with the organizing and directing power of a general diction, as I described it a few pages ago, to produce a continuous sense of orientation in the action. One is guided to the things which are most worth his attention, and guided to them in such a way that he is willing to grant that the details which the poem picks out *are* those which contribute best

---

ἑστήκει δὲ κάμαξι διαμπερὲς ἀργυρέῃσιν.
ἀμφὶ δὲ, κυανέην κάπετον, περὶ δ᾽ ἕρκος ἔλασσε
κασσιτέρου·

In it he set also a vineyard heavily laden with clusters, a vineyard fair and golden; the grapes were black, and the vines were set up throughout on silver poles. And around it he drove a trench of cyanus, and around that a fence of tin.

(XVIII, 561–5)

8.   . . . τοῖο δὲ θυμὸς
ἰάνθη ὡσ εἴ τε περὶ σταχύεσσιν ἐέρσῃ
ληΐου ἀλδήσκοντος, ὅτε φρίσσουσιν ἄρουραι·
ὣς ἄρα σοί, Μενέλαε, μετὰ φρεσὶ θυμὸς ἰάνθη.
καί μιν φωνήσας ἔπεα πτερόεντα προσηύδα·

And his heart was gladdened as the corn when with dew upon the ears it grows full, as the fields are bristling. So, Menelaus, was your heart gladdened in your breast. Then he spoke winged words to Antilochus, saying . . .

(XXIII, 597–601)

to an understanding of the action as a whole. We are faced with the almost paradoxical fact that in this kind of writing to be properly particular is to be adequately general, and vice versa. Gold is yellow and so is the vineyard as the leaves turn; but "yellow" in the description of Achilles' shield is nature and mineral at once. It suggests both the fact that the shield is an artifice and the fact that the artifice is successful in its illusion. By being in one way the expected word, it is in another way the one exact word. And being so exact in this particular use, finally, the word creates as much verbal excitement as a long poem dares permit itself—an excitement derived from the reader's sense that this kind of language at its best belongs to the individual passage and also to the poem as a whole.

A Specialized Vocabulary

Simultaneously with its concern for the meeting point of particular and general, Pope's poem is for some of the same reasons concerned with developing a suitable and particular vocabulary. I say *developing* here, because in a work as large and at the same time as narrowly oriented in its action as the *Iliad* there is bound to be something of a special vocabulary developed not only through the selectivity exercised in choosing certain important words but also through their very reiteration. We should recognize, at the same time, the shared quality of many of these words and phrases. Repetition and reiteration are, after all, not needed merely by the oral poet; they are part of the procedure of any poet who must sustain and concentrate his audience's attention for a long time. And he may hope to make his often-used words stick even better if he can exploit his reader's previous feelings about what things are named and what some particular way of naming them implies.

Pope shares a considerable number of words, for example, with one of the well-known contemporary French translations of the *Iliad*. "Char," "mortel," "coursier," "rage"—and "sage," "hecatombe," "sacrifice" in other fields of action—are used more persistently by Madame Dacier and Pope than by any of the other translators who claim to be "heroic."[9] In each case the word so nearly identical with the French is also a word familiar in its English use but not colloquial. It is not queer (Pope is very cautious in his use of odd phrases), but it is not everyday.

One has much the same feeling about such words as he has about Milton's Latinisms. Of the vehicles on which the dead are transported Pope remarks, "These probably were not Chariots, but Carriages . . . Ἅμαξα signifies indifferently *Plaustrum* or *Currus;* and our *English* word *Car* implies either."[1] But the word "car" is free to imply either meaning because it is uncommon enough in its particular use here so that we can look at it with a certain freshness. And in the same way words

9. These are of course the French forms; though *char* came over directly into English, Pope never used it.   1. *Pope's Iliad,* Bk. VII, n. xlviii.

like "etherial," "involv'd," "superior," "retorted," "enormous," which are common to Pope and Milton, mean more because of their careful use and special context than we ordinarily use them to mean. Their original Latin meaning rc-cmerges, while they remain current in the language as well.

Milton's use of this special language, furthermore, is a constant reinforcement of the main concerns of *Paradise Lost*. Something as simple as "When the fierce foe hung on our broken rear Insulting" points us through *insultans* to Moloch's identification of force with spiritual value. The defeat is insulting to him because his faith in his own power has been shattered by the attack, the "leaping-upon" of the enemy. But the two facts about Moloch coalesce in the one word; and Milton has actually given himself a valuable kind of freedom through his development of the convention. He has been able to heighten his poem in the most important way, by having it mean more at innumerable specific points and so in the whole.

There is a double value for Pope, then, in having so brilliant a use of stylization in his immediate tradition. He learns a method of having the common and repeated words in the poem seem set apart without seeming eccentric. And by his deliberate echoing of Milton he is able to suggest to his reader that he has been in the English *Iliad*'s world before. But this second value in particular involves much more than a Latinate vocabulary; as Mr. Havens has pointed out, it involves a considerable amount of direct echoing in specific phrase.

This echoing serves one obvious purpose. When we read of Achilles' helmet plumes in Book XIX, that they are

> Like the red Star, that from his flaming Hair
> Shakes down Diseases, Pestilence, and War;
> (XIX, 412–13)[2]

we remember Satan who

> . . . like a Comet burn'd,
> That fires the Length of *Ophiucus* huge
> In th'Arctic Sky, and from his horrid Hair
> Shakes Pestilence and War
> (*Paradise Lost*, II, 708–11)

This abstract shaking-down of destruction upon man is because of *Paradise Lost* already part of English heroic speech. But it also has its specific application to Achilles, as to Satan. It is not a mere adornment to Pope's poem, since it foreshadows the climax of the whole action in Book XXII.

2. Significantly, the Greek says of the helmet only
   ἡ δ'ἀστὴρ ὣς ἀπέλαμπεν
   it shone as though it were a star.
   (XIX, 381)

The brief Sirius simile in Book XIX prepares us for the more extended use of it to describe Achilles as he moves down on Troy and Hector:

> Not half so dreadful rises to the Sight
> Through the thick Gloom of some tempestuous Night
> *Orion's* Dog (the Year when Autumn weighs)
> And o'er the feebler Stars exerts his Rays;
> Terrific Glory! for his burning Breath
> Taints the red Air with Fevers, Plagues, and Death.
>   (XXII, 37–42)[3]

The echo of Milton is present again in the use of "terrific," of "burning" as the quality of a body moving through the atmosphere, and in the sequence of general curses in the last line.

The echoes in style, finally, remind us of the echo in character between Satan and Achilles and also of their parallel effects upon the worlds of their respective poems. Seeming hyperbole in the similes is literal fact for the subjects of the similes; with the death of Hector, Troy falls just as surely as, with the sin of Adam and Eve, Eden is destroyed. When Pope implies Satan behind Achilles in these passages, he defines their place in the action of the *Iliad* and keeps us by one further means from forgetting for a moment that the tragedy of the poem grows out of Achilles' power.

Dryden's *Aeneid,* unlike his fragment of the *Iliad,* maintains a consistent dignity of attitude toward its subject. It is of course an extremely influential poem for Pope, not only because Dryden was dealing with so similar a general problem but also because Virgil in the *Aeneid* had imitated so much of Homer. As a result there are many passages of Dryden's poem which can serve as guides toward a version of the *Iliad.* His treatment of certain conventional aspects of epic, too, which are still present for Virgil but have been greatly modified in Milton—the repeated epithet, the formula description, the simple animal or nature simile—is of great help to Pope in setting his own pattern of procedure with these elements of the *Iliad.*

As Pope himself points out, for instance, the death of Euryalus in Book IX of the *Aeneid* is modeled on that of Gorgythio in Book VIII of the *Iliad.* In the two English versions, as Johnson said, we get a reversal of Virgil's debt; Pope incurs it even to the rhymes.

> His snowy Neck reclines upon his Breast,
> Like a fair Flow'r by the keen share oppress'd:
> Like a white Poppy sinking on the Plain,
> Whose heavy Head is overcharg'd with Rain.
>   (*Aeneid,* IX, 581–4)

3. For the Greek of this passage, see below, p. 73, n. 7.

As full blown Poppies overcharg'd with Rain
Decline the Head, and drooping kiss the Plain;
So sinks the Youth: his beauteous Head, depress'd
Beneath his Helmet, drops upon his Breast.

(*Iliad*, VIII, 371–4)[4]

There are two purposes served here, as in the qualities shared with Milton. The similarity helps to obliterate our feeling that the English *Iliad* is merely a personal achievement; we begin to sense that for Pope as translator the various components of the tradition are as inseparable as they are for Pope the critic. At the same time that we recognize an idiom held in common, furthermore, we recognize its function in exploring a common core of human experience. We are forced by both passages to contemplate the poignancy of the meeting of youth and death; we are forced by uncommon language to a common suffering.

It is clear that this poignancy emerges so vividly in good part because of a skillfully generalized diction. But the very fact that the language is derivative, if it is also fully functional in the later poem, helps greatly to strengthen the importance to the reader of the point which the poem is making. Not only has he been in the poem's world before, but he knows that it is a world of permanently and supremely important human experience. The generalized style guides us to the crux of an individual action, but the properly used derivative style emphasizes the great recurrent crises of human life. This is evident in its most emphatic form when we consider the derivative nature of Pope's treatment of the formulas of Homer, formulas which, to repeat a remark of C. S. Lewis', "emphasize the unchanging human environment, . . . The permanence, the indifference, the heartrending or consoling fact that whether we laugh or weep the world is what it is." This pressure of unchanging reality explains in good part phrases like "watery field," "watery way," "wat'ry track," "the Main," "the Deep" (used where Homer would use "the wine-dark sea"), "the purple Morn," "the vulgar Dead"—all of them shared in some form by Dryden and Pope, and by them with other English heroic poets and translators. But in the English *Aeneid* and *Iliad* the striking thing is the consistency with which the phrases are used for precisely those aspects of the poems which depend upon recurrence and lack of change. Not only persistent nature beyond and around man but the persistent demands of human life are caught up by these formulas; and their sharing by a group of poets serves above all to emphasize the fact that

4. μήκων δ' ὡς ἑτέρωσε κάρη βάλεν, ἥ τ' ἐνὶ κήπῳ,
    καρπῷ βριθομένη νοτίῃσί τε εἰαρινῇσιν,
    ὣς ἑτέρωσ' ἤμυσε κάρη πήληκι βαρυνθέν.

And he bowed his head to one side like a poppy that in a garden is laden with its fruit and the rains of spring; so bowed he to one side his head, laden with his helmet.

(VIII, 306–8)

these basic forces are not the private property of even the greatest single poem. The conventionalized style is a way of building the immutable powers of the universe into the action of an individual poem, and at the same time a way of saying through the style how much a whole group of poems shares in attitude.

This does not, of course, mean that the style of the English heroic tradition as Dryden and Pope sum it up is a direct substitute for Homer's; indeed in the next section of this chapter we shall see how many qualities of the Greek Pope could not hope to sustain even though he recognized them as crucial in Homer's style. But the formalized language whose various aspects we have been considering is surprisingly reminiscent of the *Iliad*'s fusion of dialects which remove the poem from any one colloquial context,[5] and by so removing it make it for the reader as well as the actors a war of all men. The special language of epic is uncommon in one sense so that it may be preserved from uncommonness of another sort, so that it may be the possession of a whole culture.

The Couplet

Given the necessity for uncommonness in this kind of poem, Pope's use of the couplet for his *Iliad* may have some justification other than habit. It is quite apparent that the hexameters of Homer and Virgil are an important means of keeping the reader in the world of the poem. As C. M. Bowra says of Homer's verse, "it adheres firmly to certain rules which keep it intact and separate. If such rules had not been made, the epic might have lost much of its simplicity and rapidity."[6] And though with Virgil the hexameter does not automatically separate epic from other poetic kinds any more than the couplet of Pope does, nevertheless it is a verse which may be used for such a separation. Its distance from ordinary speech, so much more striking in Latin than in Greek, forces a listener to recognize in rhythm as in vocabulary that he has stepped out of his ordinary state. Like Molière's character in reverse, he realizes that in the heroic world one speaks poetry all his life.

In an interview prefacing a version of *Homer's Battle of the Frogs and Mice* by Pope's friend Parnell, Pope as "the Gentleman who undertook it" is allowed to express his opinions about translating the *Iliad*. There he comments on the verse in particular detail, remarking that

. . . some may fancy, a Poet of the greatest Fire wou'd be imitated better in the Freedom of Blank Verse, and the Description of War sounds more pompous out of Rhime. But, will the Translation, said he, be thus remov'd enough from Prose, without greater Inconveniences? What Transpositions is *Milton* forc'd to, as an Equivalent for Want of Rhime, in the Poetry of a Language which depends upon a Natural Order of Words? And even this

5. See Bowra, *Tradition and Design*, pp. 135 ff.   6. *Ibid.*, p. 66.

---

wou'd not have done his Business, had he not given the fullest Scope to his Genius, by choosing a Subject upon which there could be no Hyperboles.[7]

Pope's major point here is that a separation from ordinary prose by metrical means alone is not really possible for English without some serious accompanying distortion of the order of normal speech. By implication, furthermore, he asks whether one does not run a serious risk of damage to most kinds of subject in altering the sequence of words so radically. This is really what he suggests a few lines farther on in Parnell's *Battle* when he points out that "the Ridicule of this Style succeeds better than the Imitation of it."

Pope is not caviling at *Paradise Lost,* of course, but he is reminding us that Milton's famous remarks on the verse of the heroic poem ignore the difference in basic organization between English and the classical languages. And he is suggesting at the same time that Milton's uncanny success with the movement of *Paradise Lost* depends in part on his special subject matter. The evidence of the last three hundred years seems to support Pope's feeling that parody of the Miltonic style is likely to be effective, while imitation of it is likely to be disastrous. Any other poem using the style, after all, will almost inevitably turn into parody because of the gulf between the use to which at best it can put its violations of normal English syntax and the identification between sublimity of subject and artifice of style which Milton has made in *Paradise Lost.*

The syntax of the poem is, then, completely functional for Milton's highly specialized purposes; indeed its success limits it for any other use. The verse-paragraph which by its fracturing of normal construction leads us through a vast concourse of associations also envelops us in those associations. And this envelopment, in truth, is demanded if we are to recognize that though our physical world is the material of the poem it is not the poem's sphere of action. There are actually two steps of orientation. Our physical experience is transferred to the myth of the poem, we apprehend the new world of *Paradise Lost* by means of knowledge which we have already acquired; and then that myth is retransferred to our inward and spiritual life. The syntax which envelops and absorbs us furthers this transference by providing a pace which allows us to grasp the sequence. When in Book IV, for instance, Milton writes of God and the garden,

> Out of the fertile ground he caused to grow
> All trees of noblest kind for sight, smell, taste;
> And all amid them stood the tree of Life,
> High eminent, blooming ambrosial Fruit
> Of vegetable Gold; and next to Life

---

7. *Homer's Battle of the Frogs and Mice with the Remarks of Zoilus* (London, 1717), Preface, A4ʳ. Cf. Pope's "Postscript to the *Odyssey.*"

Our Death the Tree of Knowledge grew fast by,
Knowledge of Good bought dear by knowing ill.

(IV, 216–22)

one sentence, constantly twining back upon itself, provides us with an
illusion of the presence of the physical garden and also with an awareness
of its real location in moral experience. Without a break we go from the
literal trees, created for "sight, smell, taste," to the mysterious trees of
Life and Knowledge. Both are aspects of one complex experience in
the poem; and the discursive syntax plays a chief part in helping us see
how the two interpenetrate.

If a poem makes anything less than the most total demands on its
reader, however, this syntax will almost inevitably lead to bombast.
The *Iliad,* for instance, is so firmly rooted in the externally physical that
it requires a syntax which will move one through an action without im-
mersing him in it, which will maintain the illusion that he is participating
in an event without demanding that he be totally absorbed by it. Used
properly, the couplet can support a sentence structure which will maintain these qualities. The rhyme, for example, plays in Pope's work with
the *Iliad* the extremely important role of mediator between a specialized
convention of diction and a sequence of words which gives the illusion, at
least, of being normal. In a typical section of battle description,

Thus by Despair, Hope, Rage, together driv'n,
Met the black Hosts, and meeting, darken'd Heav'n.
All dreadful glar'd the Iron Face of War,
Bristled with upright Spears, that flash'd afar;
Dire was the Gleam, of Breastplates, Helms and Shields,
And polish'd Arms emblazed the flaming Fields:
Tremendous Scene, that gen'ral Horror gave,
But touch'd with Joy the Bosoms of the Brave.

(XIII, 428–35)[8]

the rhyme words guide us in the passage by their directness and their importance. Verbs or nouns for the most part, they provide us with an

8.　　ὡς ἄρα τῶν ὁμόσ' ἦλθε μάχη, μέμασαν δ' ἐνὶ θυμῷ
ἀλλήλους καθ' ὅμιλον ἐναιρέμεν ὀξέϊ χαλκῷ.
ἔφριξεν δὲ μάχη φθισίμβροτος ἐγχείῃσι
μακρῇς, ἃς εἶχον ταμεσίχροας· ὄσσε δ' ἄμερδεν
αὐγὴ χαλκείη κορύθων ἄπο λαμπομενάων
θωρήκων τε νεοσμήκτων σακέων τε φαεινῶν
ἐρχομένων ἄμυδις· μάλα κεν θρασυκάρδιος εἴη
ὃς τότε γηθήσειεν ἰδὼν πόνον οὐδ' ἀκάχοιτο.

. . . even so their battle clashed together, and they were eager in the throng to
slay one another with the sharp bronze. And the battle, which brings death to mortals, bristled with long spears which they held for rending flesh, and eyes were
blinded by the blaze of bronze from gleaming helmets, and corselets newly burnished,
and shining shields, as men came on confusedly. Sturdy of heart indeed would he
have been who took joy at the sight of such toil of war and did not grieve.

(XIII, 337–44)

articulated skeleton for the meaning of the body of the lines. The formalized vocabulary is subordinated without being lost, and what remains with us is a sense of rapid action in the passage as a whole.

This fact that some more general purpose in the poem is being served is the most important single thing to notice about the couplet. Rhyme is, of course, just one way in which the units of meaning are built by each two-line section to support and contribute to the point being made by a whole group of couplets. We have already noticed this quality as one aspect of the stamp of Pope's individuality on the poem, but it is equally important to see it as one possible way of treating the disciplined, formalized, and yet rapid poetic order demanded by heroic writing in general and the *Iliad* in particular. When Achilles in Book IX describes the future he promises himself at home, for instance, both the statement and the rhetoric of the individual couplets reach out beyond themselves to form a sustained and unitary meaning.

> Bless'd in kind Love, my Years shall glide away,
> Content with just hereditary Sway;
> There deaf forever to the martial Strife,
> Enjoy the dear Prerogative of Life.
> Life is not to be bought with Heaps of Gold;
> Not all *Apollo*'s *Pythian* Treasures hold,
> Or *Troy* once held, in Peace and Pride of Sway,
> Can bribe the poor Possession of a Day!
>
> (IX, 520–7)[9]

The repetition of one rhyme word at the beginning and end of the passage, the opposition of lines and rhymes in the second couplet, the use of "Life" both as rhyme there and as the first and controlling word of the following couplet, the idea of material treasure which binds the last two couplets into one unit which is then reflected by the last line of the passage back on the two opening couplets—all these means unfold for us a complex understanding of Achilles' weariness at this point, and in particular his weariness at the lures of the physical world which Ulysses has been

---

9.   "ἔνθα δέ μοι μάλα πολλὸν ἐπέσσυτο θυμὸς ἀγήνωρ
       γήμαντα μνηστὴν ἄλοχον, ἐϊκυῖαν ἄκοιτιν,
       κτήμασι τέρπεσθαι τὰ γέρων ἐκτήσατο Πηλεύς·
       οὐ γὰρ ἐμοὶ ψυχῆς ἀντάξιον οὐδ' ὅσα φασὶν
       Ἴλιον ἐκτῆσθαι, ἐῢ ναιόμενον πτολίεθρον,
       τὸ πρὶν ἐπ' εἰρήνης, πρὶν ἐλθεῖν υἷας Ἀχαιῶν,
       οὐδ' ὅσα λάϊνος οὐδὸς ἀφήτορος ἐντὸς ἐέργει,
       Φοίβου Ἀπόλλωνος, Πυθοῖ ἔνι πετρηέσσῃ."

"Often was my proud spirit moved to take a wedded wife there, a fitting helpmeet, and to have joy of the possessions that the old man Peleus won. For in my eyes not of equal worth with life is even all that wealth that men say Ilios possessed, the well-peopled citadel, of old in the time of peace, before the sons of the Achaeans came—no, nor all that the marble threshold of the Archer Phoebus Apollo encloses in rocky Pytho."

(IX, 398–405)

promising him lavishly. The organization of the passage, through the couplet, is really a revelation for us of the two opposed kinds of "wealth" which Achilles sees at this moment, a moment when he is closer to being a normal man than at any other point in the poem. The interlocking of rhyme and sentence is really an interlocking of thought.

Because of its power to work with the meaning of each part and yet simultaneously toward the discipline of the whole, the couplet functions like the other aspects of the heroic style. While in one way it is an abstract structure which receives its existence from those other elements, in another way its ordered variety satisfies the chief need of the style. This is so, I think, because the heroic world is pre-eminently a world without waste motion. The world of farce, its formal opposite, depends upon the triumph of irrelevance; the mock-heroic success of certain parts of *Tom Jones* results from the way in which the worlds of Homer and Mack Sennett are brought together so that consequence and inconsequence may comment on each other. But by the double comment we can see what consequence really means. Because there is no casual activity in the heroic world, the most complete result follows from every action. The true hero is equally pursued by his folly and his glory; he can shirk none of his decisions.

The chief function of a heroic style is to convey this feeling of urgency, of constant pressure and constant significance. We have seen a number of ways in which Homer does it, but the method is after all not fixed. Milton or Pope shares quite consciously with Homer and Virgil a way of looking at man, but the precise ordering of this view must vary with time and the language. And beyond all questions of the origin of Pope's style in the Homer stands the question of its ends. This is after all what we mean when we speak of Pope's interest in tradition rather than history; he is interested finally in the result rather than the source. Pope is not Homer because in order to be true to the primary fact that Homer writes heroic poetry Pope must work with the heroic mode as it comes to him. Generalized language or traditionally used diction or couplet organization is not Homer's means even though we can see strongly suggestive parallels in his own procedure. But they are ways, and for Pope the only ways, of honoring Homer by maintaining the *Iliad* in the tradition which it initiated.

5

What is the impact of his own individual style and an inherited heroic diction on Pope's treatment of Homer's Greek? In one way the asking of this question is its answer. Homer's poem takes on Pope's kind of economy and precision, the tradition's kind of order and elevation. But it remains at the same time a version of Homer's action, as Pope goes to great pains to point out in his notes ; and as he also constantly indicates there, it is one version of Homer's local effects as well. In the light of all that we have just been noticing in the style of both Homer and Pope, we must ask what happens in detail when the English and Greek meet.

There is one danger in such a question, however. We cannot know what Homer seemed like to the Greeks, any more that we can make English and Greek seem like the same language. If we are to compare the two, we must do it in terms of the significant things which are evident to us about both from our own place in European culture. Qualities which were important to Berkeley when he read Pope have vanished for us, just as qualities which were important to Plato when he read Homer have vanished. This does not mean that we must be solipsists, of course ; it does mean that our best knowledge of what has been thought about Homer or Pope at different times can assume its validity only in our own world. A proper use of the tradition will allow us to penetrate the past, but it will not permit us, any more than it permitted Pope, to escape the present.

Pope himself was constantly aware of this difficulty, of course, because it posed such special problems for him as a translator. Having accepted a duty to both times, he must somehow reconcile them to one another. But the reconciliation never allowed him to deny all the elements which could not be brought together out of Homer's past and his own present *into one poem.* He himself makes clear how many of those "alien" qualities in Homer he understood ; indeed as we compare his notes with his poetry we can see how consistently the first provides a setting for the second, a context which helps us to notice what is being done in terms of what cannot be done. Pope's world and Homer's are two sides of a triangle ; the completed translation which is the third must not only depend upon each but relate each to the other. It must recognize that Homer is alive but also that he is different.

The right means of conveying these qualities in Homer, however, will vary enormously in the annotation and in the poetic text. When he is writing the first book Pope may remark of Achilles' reappearance in Book IX,

. . . it should methinks be a Pleasure to a modern reader to see how such mighty Men, whose Actions have surviv'd their Persons three thousand years, liv'd in the earliest Ages of the World. The Embassadors found this Hero, says *Eustathius,* without any Attendants, he had no Ushers or Waiters to introduce them, no servile Parasites about him ; the latter Ages degenerated into these Pieces of State and Pageantry.[1]

We are kept by such a remark from regarding Achilles as a quaint ruler, an eccentric or a childlike king. The fairly common Augustan appeal to

1. *Pope's Iliad,* Bk. IX, n. xxxi.

golden age conditions is used by Pope here to make us think about the
real as opposed to the specious qualities of nobility—and to make us ask,
perhaps, whether our own society is not a bit curious in its interpretations
of title and degree.

But the poetry, as opposed to the annotation, must hold our attention
for Homer in another way.

> Amus'd at ease, the godlike Man they found,
> Pleas'd with the solemn Harp's harmonious Sound.
> (The well-wrought Harp from conquer'd *Thebae* came,
> Of polish'd Silver was its costly Frame)
> With this he sooths his angry Soul, and sings
> Th' immortal Deeds of Heroes and of Kings.
> *Patroclus* only of the Royal Train,
> Plac'd in his Tent, attends the lofty Strain:
> Full opposite he sate, and listen'd long,
> In Silence waiting till he ceas'd the Song.
>
> (IX, 245–54)[2]

The sense of regality is much more explicitly present than Pope's note
leads us to expect. It appears not only in added phrases like "of the royal
Train" but also in the elaborate sense of impressiveness given to the harp
and to Achilles' manipulation of it. At the same time there is no feeling
in the passage that Patroclus and Achilles have been transported from
their own context to that of Augustan England. Instead their world has
been heightened, in terms of its own kind of impressiveness, over what the
literal Greek seems to convey.

Actually this treatment of the description is only one part of Pope's
whole solution of the problem of presenting Achilles adequately, and is
best to be understood in terms of it. Constantly in his annotation he tries
to provide something of what he calls "a competent Knowledge in Antiquities"—that is, an awareness of the major cultural assumptions of
Homer's audience growing from a certain amount of factual information.[3]
But in building his poem he has also to take into account the "Antiquities"
of his own audience. For them, Achilles the embodiment of an idea is as

2.   τὸν δ' εὗρον φρένα τερπόμενον φόρμιγγι λιγείῃ.
        καλῇ δαιδαλέῃ, ἐπὶ δ' ἀργύρεον ζυγὸν ἦεν,
        τὴν ἄρετ' ἐξ ἐνάρων πόλιν 'Ηετίωνος ὀλέσσας.
        τῇ ὅ γε θυμὸν ἔτερπεν, ἄειδε δ' ἄρα κλέα ἀνδρῶν.
        Πάτροκλος δέ οἱ οἶος ἐναντίος ἧστο σιωπῇ,
        δέγμενος Αἰακίδην, ὁπότε λήξειεν ἀείδων.
        . . . they found him delighting his mind with a clear-toned lyre, richly wrought,
        on which was a bridge of silver; this he had taken from the spoil when he laid waste
        the city of Eëtion. With it he was delighting his spirits, and he sang of the glorious
        deeds of warriors; and Patroclus alone sat opposite him in silence, waiting until
        Aeacus' son should stop singing.

        (IX, 186–91)

3. *Pope's Iliad*, Bk. v, n. xxxvi.

real in the poem as Achilles the fictional person. And the idea which he embodies is in its turn a composite; it includes, of course, the blind anger he has come to symbolize, but it also includes the recognition and explication of his character by two thousand years of commentary and criticism. Pope is asking his audience to consider again through the texture of his translation an Achilles already integrated by learning with the culture of that audience.

If one were to put it in overly neat terms, one could say that Pope has had to replace a folk hero with a culture hero. More accurately he has had to replace a hero who is part of the emotional as well as intellectual culture of the Greeks with one who is highly significant for Pope's own world but who has had to be brought in from the outside and learned about. Achilles for Pope's audience is somewhat like Lear for Turgenev's; his basic significance is clear, but he must be directed so as best to evoke it for an informed but still alien audience.

Regarded in this way the great learned tradition around the *Iliad* is a measure of our distance from the poem itself; and as we have seen with the portrait of Achilles at ease, Pope must exert two kinds of mastery over this tradition. He must include it, and he must also overcome it. This double necessity appears everywhere in the poetry; as I have suggested, it is the prime assumption of Pope's whole treatment of Achilles and shows itself most clearly, perhaps, in his great opening speech.

There Achilles dwells upon the aspect of his anger which he thinks will be most influential with his audience—a denial of Agamemnon's value as a military leader and an affirmation of his own·importance to the Greek cause. It is clear that without him the Greek position is precarious, and the great oath which he takes both confirms his intention to withdraw and emphasizes to the Greeks the loss which they are to suffer through that action.

> "O Monster! mix'd of Insolence and Fear,
> Thou Dog in Forehead, but in Heart a Deer!
> When wert thou known in ambush'd Fights to dare,
> Or nobly face the horrid Front of War?
> 'Tis ours, the Chance of fighting Fields to try,
> Thine to look on, and bid the Valiant die.
> So much 'tis safer thro' the Camp to go,
> And rob a Subject, than despoil a Foe.
> Scourge of Thy People, violent and base!
> Sent in *Jove*'s Anger on a slavish Race,
> Who lost to Sense of gen'rous Freedom past
> Are tam'd to Wrongs, or this had been thy last.
> Now by this sacred Sceptre, hear me swear,
> Which never more shall Leaves or Blossoms bear,
> Which sever'd from the Trunk (as I from thee)
> On the bare Mountains left its Parent Tree;

This Sceptre, form'd by temper'd Steel to prove
An Ensign of the Delegates of *Jove,*
From whom the Pow'r of Laws and Justice springs:
(Tremendous Oath! Inviolate to Kings)
By this I swear, when bleeding *Greece* again
Shall call *Achilles,* she shall call in vain.
When flush'd with Slaughter, *Hector* comes, to spread
The purple Shore with Mountains of the Dead,
Then shalt thou mourn th'Affront thy Madness gave,
Forc'd to deplore, when impotent to save:
Then rage in Bitterness of Soul, to know
This Act has made the bravest *Greek* thy Foe."

(1, 297–324)[4]

I have quoted this passage in full because one of the striking things about
it is its operation as a unit—a complex one, certainly, but transparently

4.   "οἰνοβαρές, κυνὸς ὄμματ' ἔχων, κραδίην δ' ἐλάφοιο,
οὔτε ποτ' ἐς πόλεμον ἅμα λαῷ θωρηχθῆναι
οὔτε λόχονδ' ἰέναι σὺν ἀριστήεσσιν Ἀχαιῶν
τέτληκας θυμῷ· τὸ δέ τοι κὴρ εἴδεται εἶναι.
ἦ πολὺ λώϊόν ἐστι κατὰ στρατὸν εὐρὺν Ἀχαιῶν
δῶρ' ἀποαιρεῖσθαι ὅσ τις σέθεν ἀντίον εἴπῃ·
δημοβόρος βασιλεύς, ἐπεὶ οὐτιδανοῖσιν ἀνάσσεις·
ἦ γὰρ ἄν, Ἀτρεΐδη, νῦν ὕστατα λωβήσαιο.
ἀλλ' ἔκ τοι ἐρέω καὶ ἐπὶ μέγαν ὅρκον ὀμοῦμαι·
ναὶ μὰ τόδε σκῆπτρον, τὸ μὲν οὔ ποτε φύλλα καὶ ὄζους
φύσει, ἐπεὶ δὴ πρῶτα τομὴν ἐν ὄρεσσι λέλοιπεν,
οὐδ' ἀναθηλήσει· περὶ γάρ ῥά ἑ χαλκὸς ἔλεψε
φύλλα τε καὶ φλοιόν, νῦν αὐτέ μιν υἷες Ἀχαιῶν
ἐν παλάμῃς φορέουσι δικασπόλοι, οἵ τε θέμιστας
πρὸς Διὸς εἰρύαται· ὁ δέ τοι μέγας ἔσσεται ὅρκος·
ἦ ποτ' Ἀχιλλῆος ποθὴ ἵξεται υἷας Ἀχαιῶν
σύμπαντας· τότε δ' οὔ τι δυνήσεαι ἀχνύμενός περ
χραισμεῖν, εὖτ' ἂν πολλοὶ ὑφ' Ἕκτορος ἀνδροφόνοιο
θνήσκοντες πίπτωσι· σὺ δ' ἔνδοθι θυμὸν ἀμύξεις
χωόμενος, ὅ τ' ἄριστον Ἀχαιῶν οὐδὲν ἔτισας."

"You heavy with wine, you with the eyes of a dog but the heart of a deer, never
have you had courage to arm for battle with your people, or go forth to an ambush
with the chiefs of the Achaeans. That seems to you like death. Indeed it is far
better through the wide camp of the Achaeans to take for yourself the prize of
whoever speaks against you. Folk-devouring king, seeing that you rule over men
of naught; otherwise, son of Atreus, you would now work insolence for the last
time. But I will declare my word to you, and will swear a mighty oath on it: truly
by this staff, that shall put forth leaves or shoots no more since at the first it left
its stump among the mountains, neither shall it grow green again, for the bronze
has stripped it of leaves and bark, and now the sons of the Achaeans that give
judgment bear it in their hands, even they who guard the dooms by ordinance of
Zeus; and this shall be a mighty oath for you—truly shall a longing for Achilles
some day come upon the sons of the Achaeans one and all, and in that day shall
you in no way be able to help them for all your grief, when many shall fall in death
before man-slaying Hector. But you shall gnaw your heart within you in wrath
that you did not honor at all the best of the Achaeans."

(1, 225–44)

not a mere succession of couplets. Even more significant for us here, how-ever, are the sources of that unity in Pope's rhetorical ordering and in the traditional language of "high" action.

The chief emphasis of the Greek passage is on the individual rage of Achilles toward Agamemnon; the direct opening insult of οἰνοβαρές (You drunkard), for instance, the statement of οὔτε ποτ 'ες πόλεμον (nor ever for war) as opposed to Pope's rhetorical question in lines 299 and 300, the flat assertion of τὸ δέ τοι κῆρ εἴδεται εἶναι (that seems like death to you), all these insist on the direct personal violence of the encounter between the two. Now Pope maintains this violence, while at the same time he manipulates it toward our general understanding of Achilles— and Achilles' view of Agamemnon. The qualities of character introduced explicitly in the first line of the passage are developed in the next three and then in the following couplets restated twice in the form of antithesis. Agamemnon's failure to perform the things he demands of his men shows him both insolent and timorous in those demands. His tyranny in camp, furthermore, grows from his tyranny in the field; the aggressive desires which he should satisfy in battle are expressed only in his base actions toward his own men. As a result of all this his rule is a positive curse to his subjects; and lines 305–8 put upon both him and them a scorn which is the obverse of Achilles' pride in his own independence.

Pope has added here an ordered development; each step of the speech comes out at us as part of an organized indictment of Agamemnon. But of course the second part of the speech demonstrates that it is an equally well-organized indictment of Achilles himself. As the passage develops in English, Achilles is concerned equally with the evil which he rejects and the noble concept of freedom which he pretends to affirm.

This emphasis on a dichotomy between virtue and vice results in part from the addition of "sacred" and "as I from thee." Our attention is directed by both to the importance of the oath and to the seriousness of the split which will result from it. But even more of a controlling force in lines 309–16 is the cumulative emphasis on the oath through the scepter. Homer gets this by his description of the preparation of the scepter for its present sacred function; but Pope, knowing that he cannot depend on such a description to move his audience, works instead by emphasizing a sense of loss on the one hand ("On the bare Mountains") and a sense of judicial authority on the other. Achilles gives both emotional and legal-istic sanction to his act, and he threatens the Greeks as well.

For the introduction as early as line 311 of the fact that Achilles is go-ing to cut the Greeks off from himself throws a foreboding shadow over the solemnity of the rest of the oath—a solemnity which at line 317 breaks into a hideous prophecy. The supposed depravity of Agamemnon which has dominated the opening of the speech is played against the supposed justice and sanctity of the oath which follows; but then both taken as a unit form a background for the lurid threat with which Achilles closes. And here again Pope has added; the explicit description of a nightmare is his. "Hector comes to spread/The purpled Shore with Mountains of the Dead." It happens in this one case, of course, to be the nightmare which will take place. When we reach the madness of Book xv the seeming exaggeration of purple shores and mountains of the dead will have become matter of fact.

There is, however, another value to the diction of the concluding lines. It is completely a diction of exalted generalities, but generalities which possess the ironic possibility of becoming literally true. Achilles gains a great deal of force from the fact that he sets in his first speech the level of seriousness at which future events are going to take place. The high style of "bleeding Greece" and "flush'd with Slaughter" is actually ominous in a degree which he himself is not aware of. The end of his speech plays with vast forces, and so does the action which his speech represents; Achilles is really creating the tone here of the powers which are to engulf him. And Pope has used his stiffening of the opening of the speech to direct us toward this second application of the great oath.

What is the immediate result for the poem of such a wedding between rhetorical orderliness and stylized diction? At our first meeting with Achilles we are able to get close to him in a sense, to see the personal qualities which will dominate the rest of the poem. As in the far simpler passage where we see him at ease, Achilles and the attitude which we are to adopt toward him are set up for us in considerable detail. This is one function of the heightened treatment of the language in general; it serves as a guide into the poem's major concerns.

At the same time, however, this language makes inevitable a certain distance between ourselves and the field of the poem's action. The learned Homeric tradition and the continuing heroic tradition are not, after all, the same thing; and Pope makes the translation serve the purposes of the first as well as the second. We are kept aware of the intimate texture of an event, but we are also kept aware of its distance from our immediate world. Achilles seems familiar to us in the speech because we hear him talk in terms of the major themes which the tradition of Homer scholarship has taught us to look for. He is familiar to us *poetically* but not instinctively.

By this I do not mean to suggest that Homer has the privilege of writing without a style; but he is able to write with no apparent threat of misunderstanding between him and his audience. He does not have to guard the poem against a variety of false or partial interpretations. Pope, however, must bring together in the poetry itself what he considers to be the important qualities of the *Iliad* on the one hand and the proper guiding and informing of his audience on the other. These readers know something of what the heroic tradition has come to be, and Pope must get at them by bringing their knowledge into contact with Homer's poem again.[5]

Of course he has a variety of constantly used minor ways of re-establishing this contact. He manipulates the stock epithets so that they will not be stumbled over, and he often provides information which is implicit in the poem or explicit at another point from the one where he includes it.[6] But he has an equal variety of treatments for the Greek of the major aspects of the poem; and like his treatment of Achilles they are all directed toward the creation in the English of a consistent version of the Greek text. The similes, for instance, are shaped so as to bring out the function which we have already noticed in the Greek—a simultaneous sharpening of the precise nature of an event and also of its significance for the larger order of the poem. But the emphasis in the English is on the latter, on the relevance of an event rather than on its detail.

From what we have already seen of Pope's language in the poem, it is clear that this by no means implies verbal emptiness. In the great Sirius simile which opens the climactic action of Book XXII there is no lack of excitement, but it is excitement directed to the major issue of the book and of the poem.

> Him, as he blazing shot across the Field,
> The careful Eyes of *Priam* first beheld.
> Not half so dreadful rises to the Sight
> Thro' the thick Gloom of some tempestuous Night
> *Orion*'s Dog (the Year when Autumn weighs)
> And o'er the feebler Stars exerts his Rays;
> Terrific Glory! For his burning Breath
> Taints the red Air with Fevers, Plagues, and Death.
> So flam'd his fiery Mail.
>
> (XXII, 35–43)[7]

5. Such a statement, of course, implies a power on Pope's part which has often been questioned—his ability to come into direct contact with Homer's poem at all. See Appendix I.

6. His notes are a constant commentary on these practices; see, for instance, Bk. I, n. xxxiii; Bk. I, n. lviii; Bk. IV, n. xv; Bk. IX, n. xlviii; Bk. XI, n. xl; Bk. XVII, n. xxxv. Such annotation makes clear the tension created by the simultaneous demands of Greek and English and also the necessity for some such changes as those which Pope makes.

7.   Τὸν δ' ὁ γέρων Πρίαμος πρῶτος ἴδεν ὀφθαλμοῖσι,
παμφαίνονθ' ὥσ τ' ἀστέρ' ἐπεσσύμενον πεδίοιο,
ὅς ῥά τ' ὀπώρης εἶσιν, ἀρίζηλοι δέ οἱ αὐγαὶ
φαίνονται πολλοῖσι μετ' ἀστράσι νυκτὸς ἀμολγῷ·
ὅν τε κύν' Ὠρίωνος ἐπίκλησιν καλέουσι.
λαμπρότατος μὲν ὅ γ' ἐστί, κακὸν δέ τε σῆμα τέτυκται,
καί τε φέρει πολλὸν πυρετὸν δειλοῖσι βροτοῖσιν·
ὣς τοῦ χαλκὸς ἔλαμπε περὶ στήθεσσι θέοντος.

Him the old man Priam saw first with his eyes, as he sped all-gleaming over the plain, like the star that comes forth at harvest-time, and his rays shine brightly amid the host of stars in the darkness of night, the star that men call by name the Dog

The chief development by Pope here has been of an abstract astrological idea; Homer's Sirius is extended to include associations of a literal mad dog on one side and the fiery destructiveness of a star on the other. Ever since the death of Patroclus in Book VI Achilles has been presented by the *action* of the poem as a being whose normal nature has been maddened; the three books which precede this simile in particular have shown him struggling directly against the order of nature itself. Pope uses it as one of his many means of focusing our attention on Achilles' position by catching up at one precise point the quality of his inward nature and of his outward effect on his world. Fire and madness rage not only in his heart but also in the streets of Troy.

Seen in this way, the interpretation of the Greek is one possible fulfillment of it. As we compare a passage of Pope's with a passage of Homer's, we do not feel that the first is a substitute for the second. But I think we have a right to feel that since the second cannot exist in our language the first is *one* English equivalent. It brings the means of a particular "kind" of poetry—English heroic writing implemented by Pope's own style—to bear on the central action of the poem as Pope understands it. The English poem maintains in the immediate effect of its language a sense of what Homer is about. This is nowhere more striking, perhaps, than in Pope's treatment of the gods of the *Iliad*. We have already considered something of the general problem which he faced in presenting them to an audience alien to their serious implications; it is important to notice here the help which Pope gets from the English heroic mode in supporting those implications.

In Book XIII, where Neptune comes to the aid of the Greeks while Jove sleeps in Juno's arms, Pope has the problem of giving a sense of divinity to his first appearance where the Greek depended mainly upon his character as hero.

> Refulgent Arms his mighty Limbs infold,
> Immortal Arms, of Adamant and Gold.
> He mounts the Car, the golden Scourge applies;
> He sits superior, and the Chariot flies.
> His whirling Wheels the glassy Surface sweep;
> Th'enormous Monsters, rolling o'er the Deep,
> Gambol around him, on the watry Way;
> And heavy Whales in aukward Measures play:
> The Sea subsiding spreads a level Plain,
> Exults, and owns the Monarch of the Main;

---

of Orion. Brightest of all is he, but yet he is a sign of evil, and brings much fever upon wretched mortals. Even so did the bronze gleam upon the breast of Achilles as he ran.

(XXII, 25–32)

On p. 60, above, we have already seen some of the Miltonic implications of this passage.

The parting Waves before his Coursers fly;
The wond'ring Waters leave his Axle dry.
(XIII, 38–49)[8]

The passage in both English and Greek works in terms of a royal procession, but the Greek assumes an audience familiar enough with Neptune as a god so that it can supply the context of a divine procession as well. The English provides this context for its reader by an allusive use of *Paradise Lost*[9] and by words like "Adamant" which have simultaneously an abstract and a concrete meaning and therefore carry us beyond the physical; but above all it works by interpreting certain suggestions in the Greek about Neptune's relation to the elements.

A formalized and conventional diction is the chief means of this interpretation. "Deep," "Main," and "wat'ry Way," for instance, have their different functions in the passage; but all convey a profound respect for the sea. Like "whale's road" or "gannet's bath" in *Beowulf,* they point to the fact that the sea is not man's; it may be a watery way, but for him there is an almost frightening opposition between the two words of the phrase. Not for Neptune and his subjects, however; what for man is a force to be disciplined—if at all—by one's formal relationship to it is for them a place of play. The startling (and awkward, as of certain classes in a king's processional) playfulness of hideous creatures, the benignity of the water itself which is emphasized by the "Plain-Main" rhyme, the sense everywhere of familiarity, joy, ease where normal human experi-

8. χρυσὸν δ' αὐτὸς ἔδυνε περὶ χροΐ· γέντο δ' ἱμάσθλην
χρυσείην εὔτυκτον, ἑοῦ δ' ἐπιβήσετο δίφρου,
βῆ δ' ἐλάαν ἐπὶ κύματ'· ἄταλλε δὲ κήτε' ὑπ' αὐτοῦ
πάντοθεν ἐκ κευθμῶν, οὐδ' ἠγνοίησεν ἄνακτα·
γηθοσύνη δὲ θάλασσα διίστατο· τοὶ δὲ πέτοντο
ῥίμφα μάλ', οὐδ' ὑπένερθε διαίνετο χάλκεος ἄξων,

. . . and with gold he clad himself about his body, and grasped the well-wrought whip of gold, and stepped upon his car, and set out to drive over the waves. Then gambolled the sea-beasts beneath him on every side from the deeps, for well they knew their lord, and in gladness the sea parted before him; very swiftly they sped on, and the axle of bronze was not wetted beneath . . .

(XIII, 25–30)

This translation has some parallels to Pope, which are all the more striking because they are not integrated by any view of an English poetic idiom which would justify their use.

9. "Superior" is a fairly common word in *Paradise Lost;* both here and in VIII, 48, where Jove "smiled superior on his best belov'd," Pope uses it to strengthen the implication of a divine hierarchy. There are three more precise borrowings of phrase from Milton in the passage, of which Havens, *The Influence of Milton,* p. 580, mentions two. The huge sea beast, "enormous . . . on the deep," is from *Paradise Lost,* VII, 411–13; while "Gamboll'd" is used of various animals in IV, 344–5. "Armed in adamant and gold" occurs in VI, 110. Pope often echoes Milton in this precise way when he wants to insist on some sense of more than human dignity in a passage. Vulcan is "hurl'd headlong downward from th'etherial height," and Jove threatens the rebellious goddesses with almost the same fate in VIII, 495. (Milton describes the fall of the rebellious angels so in I, 45, where they are "Hurl'd headlong flaming from the ethereal sky.")

ence knows danger and difficulty—these create in us by the immediate means of poetry an acceptance of Neptune's divinity.

Without the use by Pope of his own techniques and those of the tradition behind him, we would not have any one sustained attitude toward the possibilities of the Greek here or at innumerable other crucial points in the poem. Actually we feel that Homer's statement and the English heroic tradition are equally alive in the texture of Pope's lines and that each is alive through the other. But the interpenetration works above all in favor of the major concerns in the Greek poem. The swiftness which Pope praises in Homer is also present in his own English; and it is so largely because his style never leaves us at a loss about where the action is headed.

In this sense the qualities of the diction, which seem so personal to Pope in one way, become in a much more important sense the possession of the *Iliad* translation. This constant concern in the individual parts for the meaning of the action as a whole keeps our attention on those aspects of the poem which Pope would never claim as his own. He has thought the poem through for himself in terms of the most adequate critical thought he can find, but then he has made his poetic skill the instrument of his best understanding.[1]

6

Pope's procedure with the verbal structure of his translation by no means explains the total effect of that structure, however. For a consistently maintained style in a long poem, even if the long poem is a translation, must do more than merely point to its original. The poetic means which make that pointing effective also create an order within themselves. As we saw with Homer in the second section of this chapter, the ordering of style is an important element in the ordering of significance; and Pope like Homer gives his *Iliad* impetus in a certain direction by the qualities of style which we come in the course of the poem to accept as characteristic of it.

One great aspect of this discipline exercised in the English *Iliad* is what one might call a "stabilizing of the unfamiliar." The generalized adjectives, abstract nouns, restrained archaisms of word form, Latinate compressions accustom us in the course of nearly twenty thousand lines to an attitude toward human action which is not the everyday one. It is not a remote attitude, but it is not prosaic; and as we have seen, its chief quality as compared with the world of ordinary experience is that one

1. See Appendix II for certain textual comparisons with earlier translations; these indicate both the kind of verbal help which Pope could hope to receive from previous work and—more important—the almost complete lack of assistance provided by earlier translators in setting a consistent attitude toward the language of an English *Iliad*.

always knows where he is and what he is to make of the situation of the moment.

There are two chief values of this quality for the poem, one of which stems from the nature of translation and one from the nature of heroic writing. We have already noted that Pope's treatment of character must constantly recognize the need for a very special sense of difference between the people of the poem and ourselves. Treated flatly and literally they would often merely amuse or repel us, so that the translation cannot pretend that they belong to our age while it must not deny their relationship to our age. But this difficulty with the characters is only one aspect of the general problem of including in current English a sequence of events which was not originally made for it. The derivative style, the high style, is a means of creating such a currency without making it common currency.

As we become in the course of the poem progressively more familiar with its particular idiom, furthermore, it ceases to be merely strange and artificial and becomes the mark of a particular world which we can accept as having something to do with our previous experience. Such a poem may be "real," but it is never realistic; it creates a cosmos where men are always in character, where each event is devoted to some great action of which it forms a part. The peculiarities of Nestor or Achilles do not concern us but rather the revelation of garrulous wisdom or prideful revenge which constantly springs from them. They are individual as they differ from one another, but they stand for something beyond this individuality. The central action of the poem shows this, of course; in the Greek as in the English it is the individual who commits an act but all society which develops the consequence.

In this way the pressure of the translator's responsibility becomes for Dryden or Pope an aspect of the pressure which the original Latin or Greek puts upon them. The core of Homer's poem, which is of permanent concern, demands the same interpenetration of specific and general which one's cultural distance from the poem also demands. For Homer's world is as clearly as Milton's one of consequence in which the reader's interest is constantly being directed to the massive and persistent through the discipline of the immediate and minute. But if an alien mind is to grasp this massiveness in a translation of Homer, it may need certain kinds of guidance which grow directly from the language of the translation.

The passages which we considered in the last section of this chapter, for instance, derive their power from the fact that they are epitomes at some particular point in the poem of one of Homer's main themes, epitomes developed through an English poetic idiom. This is a way in which the poetic translator can be consistently responsible to those main concerns of his original; and the fact that Homer creates his stylized world primarily by epithet, repetition, and simile by no means invalidates the different means which Pope and Dryden also employ. It does mean that in their effort to maintain the original *as poetry* they inevitably produce a new poem.

One specific result for their translations is a social world which is as static and recurrent as the natural world of their originals. This is particularly striking in Pope, of course, because the *Iliad* as compared with the *Aeneid* plays the recurrent world of nature so ruthlessly against the finite and individual world of man. In making the society of his translation neither present nor past Pope has modified this opposition somewhat; we find the recurrent elements in man emphasized at the expense of certain particular qualities in individual characters. Each actor seems the embodiment of a general quality; and we alternate rather than oppose the various aspects of nature and traits of man. He comes, indeed, to seem a part of the natural order rather than its dupe or enemy as he often is in the Greek.

As we noticed in our consideration of individual passages, this generalizing quality of the poem does not result in an abstract total effect. Instead it maintains a tension in the poem's major emotional crises, a tension which results above all from the interplay between formality of style and intimacy of action. In Homer an analogous effect is achieved by the use of formula-epithets for the major characters, but in Pope the feeling that we are given a double view of an action is much more pervasive. In Book XXII, for instance, when Priam and Hecuba watch Hector waiting for Achilles outside the walls, we have the utmost violence of emotion expressed.

> He said, and acting what no Words could say,
> Rent from his Head the silver Locks away.
> With him the mournful Mother bears a Part;
> Yet all their Sorrows turn not *Hector*'s Heart.
> (XXII, 108–11)[2]

The immediate and climactic horror of the event is not eliminated in such a passage, but it is muted by the sense of both dignity and inevitability which the style creates. We are involved in the action, but at the same time it is placed in a context of general and repeated suffering which is not so directly moving. We are able both to feel it and to contemplate it.

2.   Ἦ ῥ' ὁ γέρων, πολιὰς δ' ἄρ' ἀνὰ τρίχας ἕλκετο χερσὶ
τίλλων ἐκ κεφαλῆς· οὐδ' Ἕκτορι θυμὸν ἔπειθε.
μήτηρ δ' αὖθ' ἑτέρωθεν ὀδύρετο δάκρυ χέουσα,

So the old man spoke, and with his hands he plucked and tore the hoary hairs from his head; but he could not persuade the heart of Hector. The mother in turn from the other side wailed and shed tears . . .

(XXII, 77–9)

This removal from colloquial and immediate experience has indeed a general function which is suggested by passages like the one we have just considered. We are able to accept simultaneously both horror and tranquillity, just as at other points in the action we are able to accept violence combined with the intellectual control of an event, or self-pity combined with true kingliness.[3] States of being commonly assumed to exclude one another are by the style shown to be aspects of one complex experience with which the poem is concerned at a particular point. When Priam says to Achilles,

> "Think of thy Father, and this Face behold!
> See him in me, as helpless and as old!
> Tho' not so wretched: There he yields to me,
> The First of Men in sov'reign Misery.
> Thus forc'd to kneel, thus grov'ling to embrace
> The Scourge and Ruin of my Realm and Race;
> Suppliant my Childrens Murd'rer to implore,
> And kiss those Hands yet reeking with their Gore!"
> (XXIV, 626–33)[4]

we recognize that Priam himself is conscious of the paradox of his own position. In the Greek he emphasizes the daring and the pathos of his act, but in Pope's English he concentrates on the aspects of it which underlie the daring and pathos—his humility in a situation where anger would seem to be the only justifiable emotion. The outrage to him and his acceptance of it are in the concluding couplets completely balanced against one another.

Through the stylistic order of the poem, then, we are able to assimilate a richer world than we could hope to without the resources either of Pope's own rhetoric or of the immediate English tradition on which he draws. Just as Milton by his style fuses the world of Christian doctrine with the world of European cultural experience, so Pope fuses our knowledge of Homer's statement with implicit interpretation designed to persuade us to accept that statement at the highest possible pitch of importance. The particular achievements of this style which we considered earlier in the chapter are all directed toward the specific implementation of the general qualities which Pope finds most significant in the *Iliad*. But we can see now that they also and inevitably constitute a reordering

---

3. See the Dolon episode, x, 405–531, and the conversation between Priam and Achilles, XXIV, 584–839 in Pope's version.

4.   ". . . αὐτόν τ' ἐλέησον,
μνησάμενος σοῦ πατρός· ἐγὼ δ' ἐλεεινότερός περ,
ἔτλην δ' οἷ' οὔ πώ τις ἐπιχθόνιος βροτὸς ἄλλος,
ἀνδρὸς παιδοφόνοιο ποτὶ στόμα χεῖρ' ὀρέγεσθαι."

". . . take pity on me, remembering your own father. Lo, I am far more piteous than he, and have endured what no other mortal on the face of earth has yet endured, to reach forth my hand to the face of the man who has slain my sons."

(XXIV, 503–6)

of the texture of the *Iliad* in terms of what Pope can hope to make English poetry do.

In directing his style to this end, he is dealing both with a special problem of his own time and with one which concerns the makers of "serious" poetry at any time. As Sidney puts it,

. . . I have just cause to make a pittiful defence of poore Poetry, which from almost the highest estimation of learning is fallen to be the laughing-stocke of children . . . Nature never set forth the earth in so rich tapistry as divers poets have done, neither with plesant rivers, fruitful trees, sweet smelling flowers, nor whatsoever els may make the too much loved earth more lovely. Her world is brasen, the Poets only deliver a golden.[5]

Whenever we forget that poetry has as a function the creation of this special world, then it becomes a laughingstock, a plaything. The golden quality is lost as soon as we believe that poetry is not true to reality because it modifies the brazen world. A philosopher like Hobbes or Herbert Spencer codifies such a belief, of course, when he binds his sense of reality to experimental data; the data of poetry become in such a system mere decoration—they may turn golden but only as ornament.

Seen from a different point of view, however, the technical achievement of poetry, its ornament in one sense or another, has a chief justification in the cosmos made. The interpenetration of particular and general, of conventionalized and original—in Jove's love-making to Juno, for instance, "Glad Earth perceives, and from her Bosom pours/Unbidden Herbs, and voluntary Flow'rs"—guides us to the interpenetration of value and action. What we call mere narrative does not exist in language; and Pope like Homer makes this fact explicit and consistent by manipulating so carefully the relation between the thing told and the manner of telling. As a result the importance of his style exists ultimately in terms of what it does for the poem rather than in terms of its differences from our common idiom.

We must, indeed, accept the ordering of style as a standard of value for any poem, if we mean to take the poem at all seriously. The seventeenth-century "dissociation of sensibility" of which Eliot and Willey speak has its real menace in the assertion that one cannot reach valid conclusions from "secondary" experience, the experience of the world of the senses. Poetry is then split into generality and decoration; and one judges its validity by referring the generalizations to an externally held standard. Pope is still resisting this separation, however; he is minutely careful about his manner because, if he allows his tone to fracture, he will allow his readers to break out of the world of the poem and no longer accept its terms—that is, take it seriously *as poetry*. For poetry must both depend upon the immediate world and modify it—that is, give us simul-

5. Sir Philip Sidney, "An Apology for Poetry," *Elizabethan Critical Essays*, ed. G. C. Smith (Oxford, Oxford University Press, 1937), I, 151, 156,

taneous awareness of the precise event and of the order within which it has meaning.

The style of Pope's translation may then be equally a servant of the heroic tradition and of poetry itself. For just as the precise and technical means of poetry make a completed poem only if they create coherence both within and beyond it, so a literary tradition is alive only when its precise means—the individual works—stand in a coherent relation to one another. The crossroads of particular and universal within a heroic poem may also be a crossroads of individual and shared meaning within a group of heroic poems, and this by virtue of the very qualities which lend any given poem in the group its power. We have seen how Homer's statement and the English heroic speech fuse ; now we must see how that fusion is put at the service of a possible development of Homer's total meaning in terms of what the heroic attitude had come to include between his time and Pope's. If style makes a world, we must ask how that world relates to others which have already been made. And, though we accept without question the fact that Pope's poem will not stand comparison with its original, we must ask how it maintains a life apart from Homer but constantly related to Homer in its meaning as in its language.

III

Tradition and Meaning

I

IN THE PREVIOUS chapter we saw two aspects of Pope's style as most significant for the poem as a whole—that which stems from the nature of heroic writing and that which stems from the possibilities of English poetry. The two taken together create a consistent language within which the statement of the Greek poem may be developed. At the same time they suggest, through the participation of style in meaning, the further problem of the place which Pope's poem as a whole occupies with respect both to the general attitude behind heroic poetry and to that in particular behind English heroic writing. But this problem can be dealt with only if we have some specific information about the relationship of the various poems which form the European heroic tradition. As we have seen, Pope is dealing with a Homer who comes to him not only directly through the *Iliad* but indirectly through Homer's influence on Virgil and that of both Homer and Virgil on Milton. In re-approaching the *Iliad,* then, he may very well do it in terms of the living relationships which have already been established in the general ends of heroic poetry as in its particularities of style.

The *Iliad* develops as its central theme an interrelationship between two constant human concerns: the proper life to lead in the face of inevitable death, and the fit relation between men in a society. The first of these is a concern of the simplest epic poetry, the second a sign that our world of endless human complications was of central importance for Homer as it was not in the same degree for the author of *Beowulf* or *The Song of Roland.* The two problems are seen in the person of Achilles as inseparably bound to one another as they are in Ahab or Pierre Bezuhov.

In *Beowulf* or *The Song of Roland* a central interest seems to be the relentless affirmation of a way of life which will make mortality acceptable.[1] In both poems we can see the primary heroic assumption and conclusion about the value of individual life. The constant presence of death dominates both poems, and yet the hero as constantly exposes himself to death. Both Roland and Beowulf insist upon the extreme position, the

1. By this I do not mean to imply that such an affirmation is the sole or perhaps even the chief concern of either poem. From one point of view treachery and revenge dominate *The Song of Roland;* and the various possible relationships between a leader and his people are the most recurrent interests of *Beowulf.*

action of greatest danger, the rejection of aid outside themselves. They constantly test their own transitory lives.

They do not do this because common sense and prudence are unknown to the worlds of the poems. Hygclac at one point and Oliver at several explain the claims of a sensible caution, but such prudence is irrelevant to the chief characters. They are rash because they deny that caution has any serious relation to a satisfactory life. Their way of glorifying life is to force it constantly into contact with death; it is valuable only if treated almost with contempt. In a crude way their attitude is parallel to the Christian "He who would save his life shall lose it," and to indicate the similarity is not blasphemous because their justification for the loss of individual life is so definite and codified as to be part of a religious devotion.

In *The Song of Roland* this devotion is explicit, of course; Roland feels that Christianity demands the sacrifice of his life. Yet the other characters in the poem do not feel the need of so extreme a position; and he is more "heroic" than they simply because he insists so violently upon the necessity of the risk he takes. It is not primarily because he is a Christian that Roland casts his life away so gloriously and so fruitfully;[2] but Christianity gives him a superb justification for the casting away. It gives constant support to the belief that life is worth living only under certain conditions and also to the conviction that since death must come anyway it should come in a proper form—a form which will justify life by making an offering of it.

In Roland's decision, indeed, we can see a basic aspect of the meaning of Christ's paradoxical statement. Roland does not want to die, but he wants far less to live in the wrong way. And the wrong way is the way which would husband something eventually to be yielded up in any case. Roland sees the yielding in Christian chivalric terms; he offers his gauntlet to God. But the conviction of the necessity of sacrifice is an awareness not confined to Christianity.

Roland understands at Roncesvalles what Beowulf or Sarpedon also understand; the certainty of death alters the use which we might otherwise make of life. Beowulf is not eager to run the risk of combat with the dragon, since he is convinced that he must die in the fight. In comparison with his statements at the end of the poem his earlier remarks about the possibility of being killed by Grendel or his mother seem gay boasts, glorifications of his bravery in facing danger rather than conviction that he will probably succumb to it. And yet of course Beowulf's death in the dragon fight is a fulfillment of that earlier and gayer warning. He has based his whole life on the belief that one must act beyond the demands

2. A truly successful conclusion of the war is assured by Roland's death, as by that of Patroclus in the *Iliad;* the rage of Charlemagne and Achilles seems to be the one force which can resolve to a decision the balance of power with which both poems begin.

of prudence; knowing death, one must make his decisions as though death did not exist. This is the only way in which death itself is made truly tolerable.

The man who fully accepts this realization is accepting along with it a responsibility for other men. He is devoted beyond his own powers to the facing of danger, and also beyond his own needs. It is, indeed, this kind of devotion which makes Roland's battle convincing for us. We know his act to be foolish in a way, but at the same time we are made aware that his foolishness represents a more wholesome attitude than that of excessive prudence. Roland's personal folly is actually a supremely wise offering of himself to the cause of the universal hierarchy within which he lives and acts. He has one particular responsibility, which he fulfills; that he dies in the fulfillment only makes it more complete. Life is not a static possession, but a constant series of choices out of which can grow some adequate human pattern—a pattern based upon devotion of the self rather than to the self. Beowulf's eagerness that his people profit by the dragon hoard is an aspect of this devotion, of course. His death in combat with the dragon is the greatest example of a standard which he has applied to the whole course of his life; now in his final acceptance of that standard he wishes to reinforce the devotion to others which has always animated it. It is this, indeed, which the Geats recognize in refusing to keep the treasure. From Beowulf's point of view the treasure confirms the fact that his death is a final offering to his people, while from their point of view it is irrelevant because what they have lost in him is an embodiment of selfless generosity infinitely more valuable than the mere physical proof of it which the treasure represents.

None of this devotion implies that the epic hero is personally unmoved by his own exploits; it does suggest that he could be leading a perfectly adequate life in many ways without the responsibilities upon which he insists. As Achilles says to Agamemnon,

> "What Cause have I to war at thy Decree?
> The distant *Trojans* never injur'd me.
> To *Pthia*'s Realms no hostile Troops they led;
> Safe in her Vales my warlike Coursers fed."
> (*Iliad*, I, 199–202)[3]

When Achilles joys in his own honor, we must remember that for over nine years it has been honor derived from the help he gives another man. Because he is a special case, indeed, he really has no other way of deriving

3.   "οὐ λὰρ ἐγὼ Τρώων ἔνεκ' ἤλυθον αἰχμητάων
δεῦρο μαχησόμενος, ἐπεὶ οὔ τί μοι αἴτιοί εἰσιν·
οὐ γὰρ πώ ποτ' ἐμὰς βοῦς ἤλασαν οὐδὲ μὲν ἵππους,"
"I did not come here to fight because of the spearmen of Troy, since they are not at all at fault toward me. They never harried in any way my cattle or my horses."
(I, 152–4)

it; and the tragic action of the *Iliad* starts when he decides to cease making use of his gift, his talent, and begins to consider a life which will not put the most extreme pressure upon him.

The *Iliad,* then, assumes the nature of personal honor as *Beowulf* or *The Song of Roland* presents and develops it. Indeed until the opening of the poem Achilles has been acting like Beowulf or Roland; in Book I he collapses spiritually. He begins to fancy not only that there is something for him in a life without struggle[4] but even more disastrously that honor is something which may be offered directly to a man rather than something which results from offerings he himself has made. Achilles tries to substitute the secondary aspect of honor—its outward sign—for the primary discipline which is its chief meaning. Like Satan in *Paradise Lost,* he decides to make himself indispensable through his power to demand and ruin rather than through his power to support and create.

By this reversal of standards he sets in motion a series of actions which destroy not only his dearest friend but also a host of Greeks and Trojans. He feels that his refusal to continue with an actively honorable life is a justified expedient for re-establishing the proper relation between him and the other Greeks. He forgets, however, that though he is a god among men he is not a god among gods. He cannot foresee the full consequences of his selfish demand, nor can he escape them. Zeus warns us in Books VIII and XV what the outcome will be; Achilles' perverse decision must have consequences so terrible that they force him to admit his own limits and return to his proper pattern of action. He must be brought to recognize that, whether he wills it or not, he is part of the complex general destiny which the whole action of the poem develops. He must be brought to realize that his false assumptions about honor are as much an instrument for the fall of Troy as his devotion would have been.

He is given two chances after Book I to remedy his error, however. Agamemnon is sensible enough to confess his fault almost immediately after its commission. But Achilles rejects both the embassy which makes this admission and the appeal to his heart by Patroclus. By his second rejection he substitutes and sacrifices Patroclus for himself and in doing so makes an irrevocable commitment to disaster. Then at Patroclus' death he discovers that he has robbed himself not only of his dearest friend but also, through that loss, of his own power to be satisfied in meeting death. The pattern of short life and great kudos may still be his; but through his failure to understand the pact which he made in choosing that life, he has destroyed its value for himself. He has tried to deny the hard conditions of being a hero, to discover that he can free himself from them only by renouncing heroism completely. He must not hope to experiment with the demands of his position; his fragmentary view of honor is like the whoremonger's view of love, and the same disastrous

4. IX, 516–49 in Pope's version.

loss is the result. Both honor and love, he learns, are terms of devotion rather than of acquisition.

The action of the *Aeneid* is not based upon a division between the hero's potentialities and some sudden tragic limitation of them. Instead the pattern of the *Odyssey* is richly used; the symbolizing of individual human destiny in terms of a voyage, a journey through terrible vicissitude, is extended to include the destiny of a nation and a world. Aeneas is forced to a duty far beyond his individual concern in contrast with Odysseus who had struggled against superhuman odds in order to achieve the most completely "normal" ends.

Much more than the motivation is altered, of course. While certain similarities must chiefly concern us here, it might be mentioned that the individual trials undergone by Odysseus and Aeneas are completely different in their relevance to the two characters. The Cyclopes, for example, create a terrible crisis for Odysseus. In Polyphemus' cave he makes a great demonstration of his talent, and one of the greatest shows of his limitation. The consequences of the boast there dog him from that time on. For Aeneas the land of the Cyclopes is one of deprivation and terror but not of immediate concern. The giants stand impotent, while they evoke in the reader's mind the whole monstrous action in the cave. And such an evocation is used by the *Aeneid* to suggest the still unknown burdens to which Aeneas is sailing.[5]

These burdens all depend, in fact, upon a constant pressure of the unknown. Odysseus is driven during his wanderings by a perfect articulation of duty and human desire; his wish for home is as great as the need which his family there has of him. But Aeneas has no idea what the actual fulfillment may be of those prophecies about his future. He is shepherded by fate, but still he is insecure in all of his human feelings. It is these feelings which his eager acceptance of a place at Carthage insists upon and which give much of its poignancy to the Dido episode. Aeneas admires Carthage so obviously, and assists with such zeal in its further construction, because it is the ideal substitute for that unknown founding to which he can no longer urge himself. In Carthage he finds a human love and all the royal delights left burning with Troy. And it is also a logical summation of those partial attractions which have appeared in the cities he has already visited. The completeness of its appeal makes it, indeed, a foreshadowing of the destined city—a foreshadowing distorted toward comfort, familiarity, security. In terms of the *Odyssey* again it arouses all the desires of Ithaca but fuses them with the temptations of Phaeacia, Circe's island, and Ogygia.

The dilemma of Aeneas combines the problems of Odysseus and Achilles. Like the former, he must find his home in the face of fabulous

5. Scylla and Charybdis are menaces to be avoided; Aeneas' stature will not be advanced by daring them, nor will the cause for which he lives.

difficulty; he is to act constructively in opposition to vast forces of destruction. And like Achilles he must renounce many pleasures of the normal man. Wife and father are taken from him while his new love is condemned by the gods. Where Odysseus had made his own choice about going home, Aeneas' course of action has been set for him—just as has that of Achilles, if the latter remains at Troy. He must excel there and die, just as Aeneas must persevere beyond his desire and for ultimate purposes in which he will be a participant no more than Achilles at the fall of Troy.

Odysseus exceeds normal human limits in the extent and final success of his wanderings over the sea. That is the reason for his propitiatory journey—the founding of the inland worship of Neptune which is planned for him during his visit to Hades. His success is also the reason for the punishment of the Phaeacians; Neptune is outraged at this final victory over the sea of a man who has already done so much unaided. All of this is personal achievement, however; in the *Aeneid* the demands made upon the hero are part of the same vast destiny which doomed Troy. And Aeneas has the problem of living up to this destiny; he is the instrument chosen to pattern the world anew. As such an instrument he is in a position exactly opposite to that of Odysseus; he must atone for the "weakness" shown when he *fails* to exceed human limits.

Through his dedication, says the *Aeneid,* a man may go beyond the allotted mortal bounds without fear of destruction by his own prideful blindness. But if he is to do so, each rigorous condition must be fulfilled; Achilles can never yield to the merely normal, and neither can Aeneas. Each man at his best has the burden of godlike action, while he also has certain of its privileges; as Aeneas is shown in Book VI, he is not only the child of gods but the ancestor of gods. This does not alter his personal mortal nature, however, while it shows us that that nature is of value chiefly in making him willing to accept burdens so much in excess of his seeming strength. Actually it is his power of acceptance which makes him able to achieve, but he can only discover this through committing himself to the task. Aeneas really faces the central problem of belief; he can be sure that his faith is justified only by having faith. He brings about the end in which he believes, but he is never permitted any concrete assurances about it.

As one part of the value of the tradition for the *Aeneid* is the understanding which it gives us of the nature of the dedicated man, so another is our understanding of the relation between doom and creation. The *Iliad*'s insistence on the destruction of Troy is echoed and extended by Book II of the *Aeneid* to help us see both the human suffering and the divine necessity which support the founding of Rome. As the ways of the gods are not men's ways,[6] so are their true pleasures and purposes not

6. See Mackail, *Lectures,* p. 34; and cf. Helen's remark to Hector, *Iliad,* VI, 354–8

those of men. The doom of Troy is for the gods antiphonal to the fated rise of Rome, but from the human point of view the two often combine. Through the suffering of those in Italy who are forced to resist this new founding we come to understand the irony of the combination most clearly; but it is also a great part of the appeal which Aeneas himself has for us.

In him fall and rise meet, and the truly glorious nature of his sacrifice results from his willingness to participate in a building of Rome which constantly reminds him by its trials of the burdens and tragedies already experienced in the fall of Troy. Sacrifice of the innocent is as inseparable from the creation of new excellence as it is from the righting of old wrong. It is suffering which Aeneas knows best, and the constant awareness of its complexities makes him as a warrior alternately gentle and frenzied.

This quality of his nature is an enrichment and reorientation of the epic hero; but the *Aeneid* as a whole is distinguished by a richness in the kinds of material used as well as in the means of using them. The presence of Dido is paralleled by nothing in Homer or Apollonius. She is, indeed, seen through our understanding of those others who have lived on the periphery of heroic action—Helen, Nausicaa, Hypsipyle. In Virgil, however, she is truly involved with the hero even though she cannot be a part of the life he must lead.[7] As a result the whole nature of irremediable suffering is thrust into great prominence in the poem; our personal sympathy for Dido is used to indicate the emotional tenor of the sacrifice which Aeneas makes. Her pain cannot be mitigated without even greater maladjustment of another sort; and in this sense it is the inescapable suffering of Andromache as well as the lure of Helen which foreshadows the tragedy of Dido.

The particular power of the *Aeneid* seems indeed to grow from its inclusion of tragedy as part of the texture of human hope. The cosmos of the *Iliad* presents moral responsibility as the dominant aspect of the basic epic concern with a proper human acceptance of mortality. The *Aeneid* adds to this an awareness that human despair is a part of human creativity. The sense of change and alteration in the poem, so brilliantly discussed by Lewis,[8] points ultimately to an identification of suffering and combined faith as the particular wisdom of mature humanity. As time future becomes time present and as the joys of his early maturity are borne away into the past, Aeneas learns that the satisfaction which remains is the result of burdens endured rather than of pleasures gratified.

Significantly related to both Pope and the *Iliad*, *Paradise Lost* is even more explicit than the *Aeneid* about the fusion of tragedy and hope in

---

in the Greek, as well as Odysseus' warning to Amphinomus, *Odyssey*, XVIII, 130–7.

7. As a ruler, Dido does the one thing which Aeneas knows he must never do; she sins against her people by acting as a private individual, and when she is recalled to her position by Aeneas' example she rejects a responsible relationship with them.

8. Lewis, *A Preface to Paradise Lost*, pp. 32–38.

human experience. The central modification of the heroic tradition in *Paradise Lost* is the development of a new attitude to man which combines the sense of bondage to a pattern with an insistence on freedom of individual choice. Adam and Eve have as important a relation to the central concerns of God as does Aeneas. They are indeed created in order to satisfy a divine need.[9] But where in the *Aeneid* the sense of personal will is subordinate to the poem's interest in the ends achieved through a renunciation of the will, in *Paradise Lost* the question of the proper use of freedom dominates the poem's action. Where in the *Aeneid* suffering is the inevitable condition of the great achievement to which Aeneas submits himself, in *Paradise Lost* it is the result of exploring freedom. For human beings tragedy is constantly present because they are unable adequately to discipline their use of the privileges which they cannot renounce.

Paradise Lost, like the *Odyssey,* develops the nature of the normal. But it is a different norm from Homer's; and it stems in part, not from Homer but from the more than normal responsibility which is put upon Aeneas. In the *Aeneid* commonplace men may escape the terrifying responsibilities which Aeneas learns more and more fully to accept. But in *Paradise Lost* none can escape them; they finally develop into the poem's chief way of defining humanity. The pervasive sense of development points to this; Adam may think in Book iv that he has only "this one, this easy charge," but by Book ix he has learned how to interpret Satan and the Tree more adequately. And this learning is precisely proportioned to the necessary choice he faces. It gives substance and conviction to the choice, indeed; because Adam grows in understanding we accept the fact that he cannot escape decision. The sense of change which was the pressure upon Aeneas is the pressure within Adam.

The emphasis in *Paradise Lost* is as a result not so much on what is chosen as on the powers and impulses which make for a right or wrong choice. While Adam and Eve taken as a unit are in one way the chief representatives of this choice, in another way the constant dilemma of humanity is suggested through the natures of God-Christ and Satan. Both of them are vitally concerned with Adam, and they represent the character of his choice as he himself cannot yet either see or represent it. While in his world they are outside man, for us as readers of the poem they are the most generalized way of revealing to us what constantly takes place within man.

The technique of presenting these aspects of man is completely different, of course. Satan the psychological and dramatic symbol creates in his own person the self-destructive nature of the pride upon which he

9. Clearly they do not occupy this position in the theological order of the poem; but though God is complete without them, certain of his attributes can be realized only through their independent and therefore freely given service.

insists. God is either a mystic symbol—notably in Book v, where He exists in the adoring lights placed before Him—or a sequence of assertions.[1] His speeches are not dramatic but expository; they state the divine yearning toward finite beings who may freely worship or freely withhold their worship. Through such statements we are reminded again that our choice is of transcendent importance and that it always rests with us to choose—a reminder which each reader of the poem has struggled at times to deny against the constant affirmation of his experience with other men.

But the quality of the chief contenders is only one way in which *Paradise Lost* evokes the perennial human conflict. The intimacy of Raphael with Adam, for example, shows us the importance of man in the universe, while the warnings which increase as Raphael comes to understand Adam's nature prepare us for the latter's double defeat in Book ix. Raphael is no mere Hermes; he comes to tell what man may do, not merely what necessary plan God has for man. He is a part of the enormous structure which is built around man, but he demonstrates that the character of the rest of the universe cannot be dissociated from what takes place within man.

It is Raphael who describes the chain of being within which man may rise and which he must damage if he falls; it is Raphael who warns, "Accuse not Nature, she hath done her part." But a sense of the unity of the physical, human, and spiritual universe is everywhere in the poem. It justifies the special cosmos used by Milton, and it even supports the hopes of Mammon for a future in Hell.[2] The cosmos of the poem asserts a fused freedom and responsibility which we ordinarily experience only in a local and partial way. Adam and Eve alter the physical universe by their fall; but Milton is saying something much more immediately crucial to experience than that their universe is constructed to change as they change. He is utilizing the universal human awareness that as man changes he cannot help stating that change in terms of the universe around him. Indeed man is "objectively" correct in stating it so; we have no way of describing the object observed without the observer. After their bid for godhead Adam and Eve cannot hope to see the lion and the lamb lie side by side.

It is most important to notice, however, that the poem's emphasis is not on the opposition between Adam and Eve on the one hand and the suddenly savage brute creation on the other. Instead it is on their responsibility for the state of nature; the opposition between man and the physical world, which is so constantly evident in the epithets, repetitions, and similes of the *Iliad,* has altered to a bond between man and nature which may be for good or evil depending upon its use. And like the conception of a God who must suffer as man suffers, the natural universe of the

---

1. *Paradise Lost*, v, 711–14.   2. *Ibid,* ii, 274–8.

poem is designed to make us accept and live up to the demands of a constant inward struggle—a struggle which the last two books of the poem write as universal history but which still has its battleground in the individual heart.

In its whole direction of our experience toward its purposes, *Paradise Lost* is rather strikingly different from the earlier epics. We understand the *Iliad*'s attitude toward human responsibility primarily through the person of Achilles. He gives the illusion of being in his moral nature an individual; and then as we bring him into relation with our previous awareness of the world we become able to perceive in concrete and yet general terms the moral dilemma of many men. *Paradise Lost* on the other hand depends much more extensively upon our previous knowledge of man, which is then explored and refashioned as the poem creates its anatomy of the individual spirit. At the end we return to the same point from which we started, to our own knowledge of humanity now reinterpreted and reordered through the particular pattern which the poem has given to it. The progress of *Paradise Lost* has been in a sense circular, that of the *Iliad* from point to point.

This difference between *Paradise Lost* and the *Iliad* or *Aeneid* can be expressed in another way. In the two earlier poems the chief characters come because of the action to stand for certain general human attitudes and patterns. In *Paradise Lost* we start with a generalized understanding —our previous knowledge of the myth of the fall—which is then related to our particular experience of man at the same time that in the specific qualities of the poetry a new ordering created out of our world is used to reinanimate the outline original. When Milton uses the trading ship or London's sewers for a simile,[3] he is not merely giving to Satan's journey a bond with our experience; at the same time he is creating from our world a form for the meaning of Satan. We have as one completed whole the original story, our knowledge of its psychological validity drawn from our experience of the world, and our guided experience of the world as the language of the poem develops it. By the effectiveness with which he combines these means, indeed, Milton creates nothing less than a new myth for the old story. And it is a new myth which constantly demands of us that we bring to the poem our widest skill at everything from classical and Biblical learning to immediate verbal ambiguity. Virgil demands our reinforcement of his poem primarily by his use of an empire already formed as the constant external point of reference for an action which, among other things, develops the psychological motivation behind the forming of that empire. But Milton demands such a reinforcement everywhere, demands it like Virgil because his major interest is with the inward man; and to insist upon a complex use of ourselves in reading the

3. *Ibid.,* ii, 636–42; ix, 445–51.

poem is ultimately to put us within it so that we cannot escape its un-folding of ourselves. By the end of *Paradise Lost* the real locus of the dramatic action is within the reader.

The heroic tradition, however, is still at the heart of this new myth. Behind Milton's affirmation that the spiritual struggle, the struggle of inner discipline, is the most heroic subject matter, stands the concept of human discipline insisted upon in the epic before Milton. We do not fully understand *Paradise Lost* until we see that it depends upon a reversal of the tradition, but a reversal which asserts certain of the most important things which the tradition has insisted are true about man. For *Paradise Lost* the universe has become the greatest symbol of man's duty; man no longer combats the universe so much as he combats himself, and death represents merely one aspect of his limitation rather than a major enemy with whom he deals. But death and the human struggle are no less real; the poem of spiritual devotion, as we have already seen, is implied in each poem of physical devotion. Now the crisis is spiritual, the physical world a scene rather than an opponent. The lure is the same to which Achilles succumbed and which Aeneas transcended; the difference lies in the place of temptation. Aeneas is offered the chance with Dido of immediate earthly power, while Adam's equal temptation takes its form in the mind. Achilles fights in a war of social divisiveness, while Adam is within himself the very form of such division. *Paradise Lost* main-tains the heroic dilemma; it maintains also that "heroic" refers finally to an event within man as well as to a struggle in which man is only the protagonist.

But this conviction is only one part of the awareness created by the poem. The great affirmation of *Paradise Lost* is that the struggle within man is also a struggle beyond him. He cannot account for and encompass his own powers; in dealing with the self he must appeal beyond the self. No part of the heroic conflict is denied, while out of it grows explicitly the Christian paradox of finding self through the sacrifice of it which we saw suggested in earlier poems but with no hope there of appeal beyond tragedy. Freedom for Milton, as for Homer and Virgil to a degree, is only well used in the free dedication of the self. Learning and accepting the humility which that difficult gift demands is the Christian heroism. The means of epic remain in the poem, but as means to a new end. Out of a true knowledge of man's limit—knowledge which the whole heroic tra-dition gives us—comes in *Paradise Lost* a further consciousness of the way in which that limit has its implications beyond man. Virgil showed us the divine will as something in which man might participate; Milton shows us the human will as something in which deity must have a part. And he does so in a way which puts us at the core of the poem; as the center of the tradition has shifted, so has the relation between the reader and that center.

2

In the interpretation of Homer which his translation gives, what use does Pope make of such a shift in the tradition? The two *Iliads* share that general significance which I have already described; and they share it not only as it is developed in the person of Achilles but also as it appears among the Trojans, the other Greeks, and the gods. The chief differences between the poems, furthermore, the chief uses which Pope makes of the intervening tradition in interpreting Homer, grow directly from the central qualities of the action which they have in common.

In the double plot of the *Iliad,* the disastrous clash of pride between Achilles and Agamemnon comes at the most crucial point of the just war which the Greeks have waged against Troy for nine years. The Greeks are exhausted and dispirited, as their reaction to Agamemnon's ruse in Book II plainly shows; while they have reached at last the limit of time foretold in Chalcas' original prophecy. Troy is doomed to fall; but the weakening effect of the quarrel interferes with the destined course of events, and the city's collapse is momentarily stayed—even though ultimately furthered—by Achilles' desire for revenge. In this way the action of the poem is an interlude before the sure end of the war, an end foreshadowed by the reconciliation of Achilles to his duty and by the death of Hector.

The Greek poem makes the fate of Troy explicit, but at most points it merely implies the moral justification of that fate. Beyond the original sin of the rape of Helen there is the secret attack by Pandarus, the refusal to abide by the terms of the single combat between Paris and Menelaus, and the primordial impiety about which Apollo and Neptune tell us in Book XXI.[4] But it is the sequence of these events, pointing more and more firmly toward the future doom, which the Greek emphasizes.

Hector partakes more violently and directly of this fate than any other Trojan. Throughout the poem he is clearly the dominant political as well as military figure in Troy. His great love for the city is the obverse of this dominance; the sense of doom which at times he expresses indicates his fear for it rather than himself. As far as he allows himself personal feelings, they are for his wife and child; but these are not for more than a moment separate from his feeling for the state. Passionate as his love for Troy is, however, it does not blind him to the wrongs committed by Paris and perpetuated by his own courage.[5]

If he is, then, a man of such virtue in his perception and such courage in his acts, what justifies the constant pressure of fate upon him? Ultimately the fact that he, the best in the city, is in no position to avoid the city's evil even though he can see it. We see here again, as with Achilles,

4. 441–55 in the Greek.
5. See, for instance, VI, 326–31 in the Greek.

an acceptable pathos always at work inside the sternness of the poem. Hector must die so hopelessly because he is caught up in a general fate not originally due to his decision and yet one which his very virtue will not allow him to shirk. He rejects with scorn the weak sin of Paris, but he cannot detach himself from its disastrous consequences. He is beloved of Zeus, but he still must suffer an end humbling to his honor and death to everything he holds dearest.

Honor is indeed as complex and ironic a force for Hector as for Achilles. While pride and fate do not as fully fuse into one destructive energy for him as for the latter, he is nevertheless finally destroyed by a constant need to maintain his position, to assert his glory by battle against the Greeks.[6] The greatest gift that Zeus can grant him before his death is a temporary personal ascendancy in the war. But when we scrutinize that gift, we realize that it is a strengthening of Hector's native and fatal tendency. Zeus seems to grant his equivocal blessings only where a way has been prepared for them. The speech to Patroclus dying, with Patroclus' reply, is a direct foreshadowing of Hector's own death; it is also an important example of the way in which individual character supports general destiny in the poem. Zeus has told us that Hector is to die at the hand of Achilles; but the attitude which Hector adopts toward his killing of Patroclus makes his own death understandable and even acceptable. Fate becomes a psychological and personal force without losing any of its general inevitability.

If Hector is trapped in the noble service of an unjust cause, many Greeks are trapped by their service of a just one. Achilles forgets, among many other things, that he is by no means the only man whom the distant Trojans have never injured. Aside from the countless soldiers who die while he is gratifying his revenge, most of the great leaders are at the war as purely in the service of honor as he himself. This fact gives both distinction and poignancy to the achievements of Diomede, Ajax, or Odysseus. Without any of his assurance of supremacy, they are in conduct all that Achilles should be. Agamemnon and Hector are perhaps the particular contrasts to Achilles as leader of men; his fellow warriors are the great contrasts to him as individual hero.

Odysseus is a good example of propriety in heroic behavior, because we see him in the *Iliad* endowed with properties of mind as well as body which might partially justify the sort of action taken by Achilles. Whenever we are allowed a particular view of him he is supporting Agamemnon's cause with talents which are the superior of Agamemnon's own. Yet, even when issued a direct challenge to his bravery, his answer is directed toward their common cause rather than to mere self-assertion:

6. The single combat with Ajax in Bk. VII and the near death in Bk. XIV are almost mathematically placed reminders of an inevitable end in Bk. XXII to the course of action which Hector feels he must take.

"Take back th'unjust Reproach! Behold we stand
Sheath'd in bright Arms, and but expect Command.
If glorious Deeds afford thy Soul Delight,
Behold me plunging in the thickest Fight.
Then give thy Warrior-Chief a Warrior's Due,
Who dares to act whate'er thou dar'st to view."

(IV, 404–9)[7]

Diomede, a few lines farther on in Book IV, makes the proper relationship explicit when he in turn is challenged by Agamemnon. To a friend he says:

"Suppress thy Passion, and the King revere:
His high Concern may well excuse this Rage,
Whose Cause we follow, and whose War we wage."

(IV, 467–9)[8]

He and Odysseus are as conscious as Achilles of all that they are doing for Agamemnon and Menelaus, but their knowledge reinforces their virtue. Added to the concept of simple individual honor is a concept of fit hierarchy and great action—action so engulfing that one's private view of honor is no longer adequate to it. These others have mastered without tragedy what Achilles can only learn by means of it; they regard themselves as neither the measures nor the judges of the war. By their own commitment they belong to it, and this means that they must go beyond personal and physical courage to social and spiritual self-discipline. The *Iliad* as a whole is preoccupied not only with the simple problem of responsibility but with responsibility complex enough to demand self-subordination and even certain kinds of humility. Hector has learned to think little enough of himself so that he can sacrifice his personal life, the Greeks so that they can leave their homes as mere shadows for ten

---

7. " Ἀτρεΐδη, ποῖόν σε ἔπος φύγεν ἕρκος ὀδόντων;
   πῶς δὴ φής πολέμοιο μεθιέμεν, ὁππότ' Ἀχαιοὶ
   Τρωσὶν ἐφ' ἱπποδάμοισιν ἐγείρομεν ὀξὺν Ἄρηα;
   ὄψεαι, ἢν ἐθέλησθα καὶ αἴ κέν τοι τὰ μεμήλῃ,
   Τηλεμάχοιο φίλον πατέρα προμάχοισι μιγέντα
   Τρώων ἱπποδάμων· σὺ δὲ ταῦτ' ἀνεμώλια βάζεις."

"Son of Atreus, what a word has escaped the barrier of your teeth! How do you say that we are slack in battle, whenever we Achaeans rouse keen war against the horse-taming Trojans? You shall see, if indeed you will and care at all for it, the father of Telemachus mingling with the foremost fighters of the horse-taming Trojans. This that you say is empty wind."

(IV, 350–5)

8. "τέττα, σιωπῇ ἧσο, ἐμῷ δ' ἐπιπείθεο μύθῳ·
   οὐ γὰρ ἐγὼ νεμεσῶ Ἀγαμέμνονι, ποιμένι λαῶν,
   ὀτρύνοντι μάχεσθαι ἐϋκνήμιδας Ἀχαιούς."

"Good friend, abide in silence, and be prevailed on by my word. I do not count it shame that Agamemnon, shepherd of the host, should urge on to battle the well-greaved Achaeans."

(IV, 412–14)

or twenty years. Against such a background Achilles' insurrection assumes its full meaning of blindness, pride, and ignorance.

The characters of the subordinate gods bear at times a surprising
similarity to his. Some one of them is always asserting his will against
the decrees of Zeus and fate, always insisting on the possibility that
proper resolution on the part of others will render Zeus powerless. The
great difference lies in the sequel, of course; at least in the *Iliad* the other
gods always yield to Zeus before his threatened punishment, and that
punishment has never in any case the irrevocable quality of the disasters
which come upon men. This partialness of the inferior deities is of course
only one aspect of what has often been called their immorality. Actually
their behavior is intensely moral in its implications for men; the im-
mortals do all the things which mortals are often tempted to do, but they
never make a human recompense for their acts. Adultery on Olympus
is cause for laughter; on earth it causes the Trojan War. The gods are
in this way not a human ideal so much as they are an all too human dream.

In making such a statement, however, we must distinguish between
the other gods and Zeus. It is his presence which brings order into the
heavenly hierarchy, order both of a physical and a philosophical sort. His
discipline of the others indicates to us that Olympus is more than a mere
wish fulfillment; it is also the apex of a pyramid of relationships. These
relationships work not merely by prayer from men to the gods but by
interest and partiality from the gods to men. At several critical points in
the action of the *Iliad,* the gods wonder among themselves why they
waste energy on mortals;[9] but their wonder never seems to keep them
from doing so. They see the transitory nature of human life as clearly as
men do in their moments of understanding—the poem emphasizes this
by having both gods and men use the same image to describe it—[1]but
they continue to feel affection for some men, rage at others, and a passionate interest in the whole progress of the war.

Zeus feels this interest as clearly as the other gods but for reasons
which include theirs and go beyond them. The poem never makes it completely clear whether his will is synonymous with fate or whether he
automatically concurs in the fated future. But in either case he knows
what that future will be, and thus he is the only god who worries about
fitting particular events into a predestined scheme. This does not mean
that he has no affection, that he is cold and impartial. But he is usually
content, as none of the other gods is, to resign his partial desires.[2]

Being content to do so, he can see possibilities of action which the other

9. Vulcan in Bk. I and Apollo in Bk. XXI, for instance, urge the folly of wasting effort
on such transient creatures.   1. See above, pp. 35–6, nn. 3, 4.

2. Pope emphasizes this distinction by using "partial" as a constant term of reproach
between gods who disagree over the giving of favor and as the word with which they
recall Jove to himself (see the following note). See *Iliad,* I, 675; VIII, 450; and cf. Agamemnon's use of the word in II, 147; IX, 31.

gods constantly miss. At times they function in the *Iliad* very much as the angels in *Paradise Lost* do but without being conscious of their place. They are the intermediaries, the agents, those who perform the will of heaven without knowing more than a part of it at any one time. They are not the final determinants of an action but the participants in it—when they are allowed—on an enlarged and faintly foolish scale. Apollo, like Achilles, is allowed his private interest as long as it can be reconciled to a general plan of action; but neither has any influence over Zeus at crucial points in that action—when Patroclus goes to battle or when Hector faces Achilles at last.

The inferior gods are, then, not merely interested in men; they share with them a dependence on destiny. Zeus seems to be the only god privileged to debate within himself whether to accept this destiny or to do things some other way. And on two occasions when he meditates a small modification of fate in the interest of his own affections, he is quickly restrained by the arguments of the other gods. They recall him to the impartiality which he must maintain if he is to uphold general justice rather than personal desire as the rule of the universe.[3] The other gods expect these deviations in themselves, but they are surprised to find them appearing in him. This attitude on their part is of course a tacit acknowledgment of Zeus' supremacy, which may be questioned for a moment by Poseidon or Hera and Athena but never for more than a moment.[4]

Such an acknowledgment on the part of the other gods is also a tacit assertion that force alone does not rule the universe. Zeus several times threatens other gods with his strength, but behind their obedience lies the conviction that he should be obeyed because he stands for something beyond personal whim. When angry Neptune proclaims his independence in Book xv, he as quickly resigns it again with the proviso that

> If yet, forgetful of his Promise giv'n
> To *Hermes, Pallas,* and the Queen of Heav'n;
> To favour *Ilion,* that perfidious Place,
> He breaks his Faith with half th'ethereal Race;
> Give him to know, unless the *Grecian* train
> Lay yon' proud Structures level with the Plain,
> Howe'er th'Offence by other Gods be past,
> The Wrath of *Neptune* shall for ever last.
>   (xv, 236–43)[5]

3. *Iliad*, XVI, 528–58; XXII, 221–40 (431–58, 167–85 in the Greek).
4. Since Pope uses the Latin forms of the gods' names, it is impossible to be completely consistent in referring to them. I have attempted, however, to abide by the Greek whenever Homer is being discussed.
5.   "αἴ κεν ἄνευ ἐμέθεν καὶ Ἀθηναίης ἀγελείης,
       Ἥρης Ἑρμείω τε καὶ Ἡφαίστοιο ἄνακτος,
       Ἰλίου αἰπεινῆς πεφιδήσεται, οὐδ᾽ ἐθελήσει
       ἐκπέρσαι, δοῦναι δὲ μέγα κράτος Ἀργείοισιν,

He grants that Zeus is in a position to make promises to the other gods; and so does the reader, to whom Zeus a few lines later tells a part of his plan.

Agamemnon also insists on this justice, an insistence which causes many of his bafflements throughout the poem. He is right, of course; but he is often disappointed because he forgets that justice to his cause may not be at all pleasant for him personally. His attitude toward Zeus in Books II and IX is as forgetful as Achilles' of this central truth. The poem intermingles fate and justice in the person of Zeus, because the inexorability of justice is something men would always be glad to hide from themselves. It seems hard that Agamemnon should repent so quickly of his folly and yet be punished for so long through the sufferings of his army. But he, and Achilles, and just Hector, and unjust Troy, and pathetic Priam, must all fit into one pattern. It is one of the poem's great affirmations that such a pattern exists; but one can only avoid sentimentality in such an idea by affirming also that man was made for the pattern and not the pattern for man.[6] This is the lesson which the poem's chief characters learn through suffering and death; and it is the lesson which justifies presenting the gods and men in the poem as comprising one significant structure.

If such an idea of interdependence is one of the great resemblances between Pope's poem and Homer's, it is also one of the main points of difference between the two. For Pope in developing Homer's idea has bound it to certain concepts—and to the poetic formulation of those concepts—in his own intellectual tradition. Such concepts deal much more explicitly than Homer's with the way in which man is related to other aspects of the universe and the way in which this relationship puts demands of responsibility upon him. And they grow, not only from the increasing concern with the relatedness and therefore with the responsibility which we see in the heroic tradition itself but also from the medieval and Renaissance "world picture" whose vitality Tillyard and others have demonstrated for the sixteenth and seventeenth centuries.[7] There is no need here to recapitulate what has already been discussed in its various

---

ἴστω τοῦθ', ὅτι νῶϊν ἀνήκεστος χόλος ἔσται."

". . . if in despite of me, and of Athene, driver of the spoil, and of Hera, and Hermes, and lord Hepheaestus, he shall spare steep Ilios, and shall be unwilling to lay it waste, or to give great force to the Argives, let him know this, that between us two shall be anger that nothing can appease."

(xv, 213–17)

6. This is the meaning of Eumaeus' remark in Bk. xv of the *Odyssey* (400–1 in the Greek) that "a man who has been through bitter experiences and travelled far can enjoy even his sufferings after a time."

7. E. M. W. Tillyard, *The Elizabethan World Picture* (London, Chatto and Windus, 1943); A. O. Lovejoy, *The Great Chain of Being* (Cambridge, Harvard University Press, 1936); Lewis, *A Preface to Paradise Lost*; Basil Willey, *The Seventeenth Century Background* (London, Chatto and Windus, 1934), are among the most useful in explaining both what was believed and also what was perceived by means of that belief.

aspects; the striking thing to remember is that this view of a universe
of interdependent and in a sense living parts maintains its poetic validity
long after it has been philosophically stormed and indeed that it is in part
useful as a buttress against the increasing abstractness of mathematical
and mechanical philosophies. The older world view is almost demanded
of Pope if he is to maintain—as we have seen him doing in his Homer
criticism—the objective significance of poetry rather than its mere romance or decorative value.

A clear example of the use which he can make of both these major
traditions is the point in Book IV where Agamemnon laments over Menelaus' wound:

> ". . . when Heav'n's Revenge is slow,
> *Jove* but prepares to strike the fiercer Blow.
> The Day shall come, that great avenging Day,
> Which *Troy*'s proud Glories in the Dust shall lay,
> When *Priam*'s Powers and *Priam*'s self shall fall,
> And one prodigious Ruin swallow all.
> I see the God, already, from the Pole
> Bare his red Arm, and bid the Thunder roll;
> I see th'Eternal all his Fury shed,
> And shake his *Aegis* o'er their guilty Head."
>
> (IV, 194–203)[8]

Two aspects of Pope's development of the Greek are important here: the
sense of a cosmic moral judgment which he sharpens so carefully, and
the specific detail which ties this judgment firmly to our physical universe. Certain aspects of the Flood have entered in—the use of the elements as instruments of judgment, for example, and the assertion by
Troy of her proud independence from deity. Pope has developed heroic
morality beyond the Greek, while in doing so he has extended the symbolic
quality latent in the Greek.

But Pope's heightening of our consciousness of divine justice is only

8.   "εἴ περ γάρ τε καὶ αὐτίκ᾽ Ὀλύμπιος οὐκ ἐτέλεσσεν,
ἔκ τε καὶ ὀψὲ τελεῖ, σύν τε μεγάλῳ ἀπέτισαν,
σὺν σφῇσιν κεφαλῇσι γυναιξί τε καὶ τεκέεσσιν.
εὖ γὰρ ἐγὼ τόδε οἶδα κατὰ φρένα καὶ κατὰ θυμόν·
ἔσσεται ἦμαρ ὅτ᾽ ἄν ποτ᾽ ὀλώλῃ Ἴλιος ἱρὴ
καὶ Πρίαμος καὶ λαὸς ἐϋμμελίω Πριάμοιο,
Ζεὺς δέ σφι Κρονίδης ὑψίζυγος, αἰθέρι ναίων,
αὐτὸς ἐπισσείῃσιν ἐρεμνὴν αἰγίδα πᾶσι
τῆσδ᾽ ἀπάτης κοτέων·"

"For even if the moment the Olympian does not fulfill [oaths], yet late and at
length he does fulfill them, and with a heavy price men make atonement, with their
own heads and their wives and their children. For I know this well in heart and
soul: the day will come when sacred Ilium shall be laid low, and Priam, and the
people of Priam, skilled at the ashen spear; and Zeus, son of Cronos, throned on
high, who dwells in heaven, shall himself shake over them all his dark aegis in
wrath for this deceit."

(IV, 160–8)

one small part of his development of the gods. Even the briefest comparison with Homer, in the light of the other chief epic poets, shows us what he was able to develop through the two traditions. Zeus issues a warning to Hera which is echoed by the deities of later poems:

"Hector shall not refrain from battle until the swift-footed son of Peleus uprise beside his ships on the day when at the ships' sterns they shall fight most violently around fallen Patroclus; for thus it is ordained by Heaven. . . . I care not for your anger, since there is none more shameless than you."

(*Iliad*, VIII, 473–7, 482–3)[9]

"Nor shall you fail to see that city, and the proud foreordained wall encompassing Lavinium. You yourself shall bear Aeneas the great-hearted starward to the heights of heaven. Nothing swerves my will once uttered."

(*Aeneid*, I, 259–63)

"Boundless the deep, because I am who fill
Infinitude; nor vacuous the space,
Though I, uncircumscribed, myself retire,
And put not forth my goodness, which is free
To act or not. Necessity and Chance
Approach not me, and what I will is Fate."

(*Paradise Lost*, VII, 168–73)

"Nor shall great *Hector* cease the Rage of Fight,
The Navy flaming, and thy *Greeks* in Flight,
Ev'n till the Day, when certain Fates ordain
That stern *Achilles* (his *Patroclus* slain)
Shall rise in Vengeance, and lay Waste the Plain.
For such is Fate, nor can'st thou turn its Course
With all thy Rage, with all thy Rebel Force.
Fly, if thou wilt, to Earth's remotest Bound,

. . .

There arm once more the bold *Titanian* Band;
And arm in vain: for what I will, shall stand."

(*Iliad*, VIII, 590–7, 603–4)

Pope's explicitly metaphysical Zeus is fully comprehensible as a version of Homer's only in the light of the deities of Virgil and Milton. His supremacy in the English is the result of consistently applied power—the consistency presented by him under the name of Fate.

The sense of immutable pattern is made much heavier. Zeus in the

9.   "οὐ γὰρ πρὶν πολέμου ἀποπαύσεται ὄβριμος Ἕκτωρ,
πρὶν ὄρθαι παρὰ ναῦφι ποδώκεα Πηλεΐωνα,
ἤματι τῷ ὅτ᾽ ἂν οἱ μὲν ἐπὶ πρύμνῃσι μάχωνται,
στείνει ἐν αἰνοτάτῳ περὶ Πατρόκλοιο θανόντος,
ὣς γὰρ θέσφατόν ἐστι.

. . .

                              οὐ σευ ἔγὼ γε
σκυζομένης ἀλέγω, ἐπεὶ οὐ σέο κύντερον ἄλλο."

Greek poem has, as I have pointed out, a clear idea of the way in which the whole war is to go; but he considers each part of it, in his discussions with the other gods, as a single, almost physical action. When he and Poseidon converse in the Greek about the wall which has been built around the Achaean camp, Zeus' counsel is simple enough: " 'Come now; when the long haired Achaeans have gone again with their ships to their dear native land, then burst apart the wall and sweep it all into the sea, and cover the great beach again with sand . . .' " (*Iliad*, VII, 459–62). Foreboding and an assertion of the permanent forces of the universe dominate the English:

> "But yon' proud Work no future Age shall view,
> No Trace remain where once the Glory grew.
> The sapp'd Foundations by thy Force shall fall,
> And whelm'd beneath thy Waves, drop the huge Wall;
> Vast Drifts of Sand shall change the former Shore;
> The Ruin vanish'd, and the Name no more."
> (VII, 549–54)[1]

Pope's Neptune is no longer a deity fearful lest men should compare the glory of their works to his own. Through the guidance and vision of Jove, he becomes the power capable of putting the works of man in their proper position relative to the total structure of things.

More than any other single point, it is Jove's consciousness of this total structure which separates the English poem from the Greek. For Homer's men Fate is a great and constant pressure; but for Pope's gods also it is an inescapable concern. Homer's gods take a great interest in what goes on; but Pope's gods are a part of it. Their fated tasks are not tragic like those of men, but they are no more escapable than the human burdens in the poem. Like the gods in Virgil and the divine hierarchy in *Paradise Lost*—and unlike the inferior gods in the Greek *Iliad*—they have a task to perform; if in one sense, as Helen says in the *Odyssey*, men suffer in order to make a song for the gods, in another sense the gods as Pope sees them also participate in order to make that pattern possible. The human universe in Pope's *Iliad* is a thing made, and the gods for whom it is made also help to make it. The reciprocal relationship between gods and men is constantly present in the English poem because both are bound to one law.

1.   "ἄγρει μάν, ὅτ᾽ ἂν αὖτε κάρη κομόωντες Ἀχαιοὶ
     οἴχωνται σὺν νηυσὶ φίλην ἐς πατρίδα γαῖαν,
     τεῖχος ἀναρρήξας τὸ μὲν εἰς ἅλα πᾶν καταχεῦαι,
     αὖτις δ᾽ ἠϊόνα μεγάλην ψαμάθοισι καλύψαι,
     ὥς κέν τοι μέγα τεῖχος ἀμαλδύνηται Ἀχαιῶν."

"Come now: when once the long haired Achaeans have gone with their ships to their dear native land, you burst apart the wall and sweep it all into the sea, and cover the great beach again with sand, so that the great wall of the Achaeans may be brought to nothing by you."

(VII, 459–63)

This kind of law is one of the chief things which make Virgil's gods different from Homer's, of course; and it is also one of the qualities of the *Aeneid* which make it seem an anticipation of Christian ideas of order. In Pope's poem, however, the two kinds of order combine as they are reapplied to Homer. For instance when Zeus in Book I has pointed out to Hera the virtue of keeping her place, she persists in questioning his promises:

> Then thus the God: Oh restless Fate of Pride,
> That strives to learn what Heav'n resolves to hide;
> Vain is the Search, presumptuous and abhorr'd,
> Anxious to thee, and odious to thy Lord.
> Let this suffice; th'immutable Decree
> No Force can shake: what *is,* that *ought* to be.
> (*Iliad,* I, 726–31)[2]

The italics are Pope's, as is the implicit application of the passage to man on the one hand and Zeus himself on the other. The immutable decree seems to bind him as it binds everyone else; for while he wills it, he does not seem free to will caprice, evil, or inconsistency. He, like every other being in the universe, is bound by an identification between ultimate power and moral good.

That this identification provides a series of logical, metaphysical, and theological snarls does not at all modify its importance for our understanding of Pope's *Iliad*. Quite the opposite, in fact; Zeus' involvement in the justice of the decrees he wills, so complex metaphysically, is the sharpest guarantee that human lives are bound to the problem of order. As we have already seen, this problem of order, like the problem of justice, is already present in the Greek poem. What Pope has done, in providing a generalized and explicitly immutable character for Zeus, is to provide also a specific and relentless (even though not consistent) philosophical and theological structure for the lives of men—not merely a relentless series of events, as in the Greek.

This structure is suggested in the passage quoted just above. The Greek implies nothing beyond Hera's performance of a personal action; the English generalizes on this but in such a way that the generality becomes specific again for man. Hera's one act is also a common human action;[3]

2. "δαιμονίη, αἰεὶ μὲν ὀίεαι, οὐδέ σε λήθω·
    πρῆξαι δ' ἔμπης οὔ τι δυνήσεαι, ἀλλ' ἀπὸ θυμοῦ
    μᾶλλον ἐμοὶ ἔσεαι· τὸ δέ τοι καὶ ῥίγιον ἔσται.
    εἰ δ' οὕτω τοῦτ' ἐστίν, ἐμοὶ μέλλει φίλον εἶναι."

"Strange queen, you are always imagining, and I do not escape you; yet you shall in no way have power to accomplish anything, but shall be the farther from my heart, and that shall be even the worse for you. If this thing is as you say, then it must be my good pleasure."

(I, 561–4)

3. Pope creates a context for this passage, of course, by his echoes of phrase and attitude in the *Essay on Man* descriptions of man's place in the universe. See I, 281–94.

the echoes of Christian-Hebrew traditional language call our attention to this and suggest still further the kinship between the inferior gods and men. As they are bound to a common law, so they are capable of the same offenses.

Destiny in the poem is for both Homer and Pope a way of pointing to our common human blindness. Hector remarks in Book VI on the fated end of Troy but never seems conscious of any of his contributions to that fate, contributions which for the reader of the poem form so clear a pattern. "Who knows the Will of Heav'n?," he remarks as he rips the lance from Patroclus' corpse; but we have been warned by Zeus and can detect in terms of his act the sequence of events to come. As the *Iliad* treats the destiny enveloping Hector or Achilles, however, its very pressure provides them with an opportunity for freedom. The sure end of the war is created out of myriad interacting wills, each one unsure within itself and yet choosing step by step the single events which make a completed and "necessary" whole. The paradox is never completely resolvable, of course; we can say that Achilles *must* yield to his pride, because his nature demands such a yielding. And yet in saying so we are not true to human experience or to the facts of the poem. Athene in Book I is really a part of the struggle going on within Achilles; only after he has made his choice can we honestly say that he must have done what he did.

The most important distinction to make here is that between the reader of the *Iliad* and the participant in its action. One point of the poem, after all, is to show us a pattern of reality as we could never detect it in our own developing lives. We are placed in the position of gods; we see past, present, and future as one completed whole. We see destiny as a power outside any of the poem's characters; but the form of it that we know in life is also present as the constant necessity to choose. The choice is real, and yet each choice brings irrevocable consequences with it; it is part of a total fabric, one of whose names is fate. The end of the Trojan War is fixed, but the sorrow of Achilles brings it about.

As we have seen, this interpenetration of personal choice and cosmic order is explored and developed through the whole heroic tradition; and it is constantly emphasized and pointed up by Pope as an aspect of the complex social morality which he heightens in the poem. The concept of a chain of being is chiefly useful to him in his translation, as it had been to Milton, as a means of defining one possible structure of logic and imagery for this middle state of man—choosing and yet forced to abide by his choice—which is assumed by poems as different as the *Iliad* and *Paradise Lost*. The traditional association of the chain of being with

---

The technique is one which Pope uses for *The Rape of the Lock*, where the *Iliad* itself supplies the context; see William Frost, *"The Rape of the Lock* and Pope's Homer," *Modern Language Quarterly, 8* (1947), 342–54.

Homer's poem is of long standing. Lovejoy quotes a passage from Macrobius which concludes its epitome of the concept of necessary interrelationship with the remark, "And this is Homer's golden chain, which God, he says, bade hang down from heaven to earth."[4] It is also Milton's golden chain, of course; but it is most important to notice that what starts out as the allegorizing comment of a Neoplatonist philosopher emerges for a later Christian poet as a major means of supporting and enriching the action of the *Iliad* without doing violence to it.

We have noticed how the gods in Pope's poem come to be as truly involved as men in its central events. The chain-of-being idea, however, reinforces at least as strikingly the place of man himself—not only the way in which his freedom cannot be separated from its consequences but the way in which it makes constant positive demands of him. Achilles and Agamemnon, for example, are struggling chiefs in the Greek; in the English they are exponents of the complex problem of rule. Thersites is a monstrous person in the Greek; in the English he is also an example of the sin against order which Juno, Mars, and Neptune at times show in heaven. Ulysses is not only conscious, as in the Greek, of place and hierarchy among the members of a society, he is a constant and explicit symbol of the nature, obligations, and value of noble behavior. He is supremely aware of the problem of order; he is also its constant spokesman and exemplar throughout the poem.

These qualities appear nowhere so fully concentrated, perhaps, as in his encounter with Thersites in Book II. There, where offender and champion meet, Pope has given in part his poetic realization of the *Iliad*'s "chief Moral" according to him, "that Concord, among Governours, is the preservation of States, and Discord the ruin of them." By doing so he of course furthers the plot of the poem since we are reminded again of Agamemnon's error and also of the greater sin of Achilles. But more important is the interrelationship upon which Pope's Ulysses, like Shakespeare's, shows the concord of states, or universes, to depend.

This starts in a most immediate way with Thersites, "His Figure such as might his Soul proclaim . . ." The physical is a foreshadowing of the intellectual and spiritual:

> Spleen to Mankind his envious Heart possest,
> And much he hated All, but most the best.
>
> (II, 267–8)[5]

---

4. Lovejoy, *The Great Chain of Being*, p. 63, n. 53.

5. It is impossible to give the Greek for this couplet, since Pope created it from suggestions in a somewhat longer passage whose explicit statements he also presents:

> ἔχθιστος δ' Ἀχιλῆϊ μάλιστ' ἦν ἠδ' Ὀδυσῆϊ·
> τὼ γὰρ νεικείεσκε· τότ' αὖτ' Ἀγαμέμνονι δίῳ
> ὀξέα κεκλήγων λέγ' ὀνείδεα.

He was hateful to Achilles above all, and to Odysseus, for it was those two that

This spleen expresses itself, of course, in a vilification of Agamemnon which implies both praise of himself and denial of the structure of the state. Thersites is echoing Achilles' statements but without the partial justification which Achilles' stature granted for his anger.

> "What'er our Master craves, submit we must,
> Plagu'd with his Pride, or punish'd for his Lust.
>
> .   .   .
>
> We may be wanted on some busie Day,
> When *Hector* comes: so great *Achilles* may:
> From him he forc'd the Prize we jointly gave,
> From him, the fierce, the fearless, and the brave:
> And durst he, as he ought, resent that Wrong,
> This mighty Tyrant were no Tyrant long."
> (ii, 291–2, 296–301)[6]

Ulysses recognizes that the vocabulary and the person are violently incongruous, and he recognizes also in his rebuke the direction of Thersites' chief threat.

> "Peace, factious Monster, born to vex the State,
> With wrangling Talents form'd for foul Debate:
> Curb that impetuous Tongue, nor rashly vain
> And singly mad, asperse the sov'reign Reign.
>
> .   .   .
>
> For our Return we trust the heav'nly Pow'rs;
> Be that their Care; to fight like Men be ours!"
> (ii, 306–9, 314–15)[7]

---

he was accustomed to revile; but now again with shrill cries he uttered abuse against goodly Agamemnon.

(ii, 220-2)

6. "οὐ μὲν ἔοικεν
ἀρχὸν ἐόντα κακῶν ἐπιβασκέμεν υἶας Ἀχαιῶν.

. . .

ὄφρα ἴδηται
ἤ ῥά τί οἱ χὴμεῖς προσαμύνομεν, ἦε καὶ οὐκί·
ὃς καὶ νῦν Ἀχιλῆα, ἔο μέγ' ἀμείνονα φῶτα,
ἠτίμησεν· ἑλὼν γὰρ ἔχει γέρας, αὐτὸς ἀπούρας.
ἀλλὰ μάλ' οὐκ Ἀχιλῆϊ χόλος φρεσίν, ἀλλὰ μεθήμων·
ἦ γὰρ ἄν, Ἀτρείδη, νῦν ὕστατα λωβήσαιο."

"It is not fitting for their leader to bring to evil the sons of the Achaeans. . . . [Let us leave him] so that he may learn whether there is in us too anything of help for him or not—for him who has now done dishonor to Achilles, a man far better than he; for he has taken away and keeps the prize by his own arrogant act. Certainly there is nothing of anger in the heart of Achilles; no, he heeds not at all; or else, son of Atreus, you would now work insolence for the last time."

(ii, 233-4, 237-42)

7. "Θερσῖτ' ἀκριτόμυθε, λιγύς περ ἐὼν ἀγορητής,
ἴσχεο, μηδ' ἔθελ' οἶος ἐριζέμεναι βασιλεῦσιν.

. . .

Thersites has attempted to set himself up in judgment against the whole fabric of the state. No man has a right to do this, Ulysses implies; that is the point of his insistence that all the Greeks leave the larger plan of action to the care of the gods. That Achilles is angry at Agamemnon is no justification for his denial of the "sovereign Reign"; the least and the greatest of the Greeks meet in this, that both have violated the structure of things, have directed themselves to a part rather than the whole.

Pope has implied here, as at many other points in the poem and in many different ways, the form of a general situation in a particular event.[8] This is perhaps his greatest single difference from Homer who, as we have seen with the gods, tends to treat his generalities directly as particulars. The complex ordering of the tradition behind Pope provides the means for placing his translation at a meeting point of the general and the particular, and at the same time almost demands that he place it so, if he is to do his best for Homer in terms of his own standards of critical excellence. Milton's hierarchy of nature is inseparable from his concept of responsible man; in *Paradise Lost* they are two extremes in a whole complex which is concerned with the discovery of man's participation in the ultimate forces of the universe. Pope cannot ignore that redirection of interest in the tradition except by rejecting it as a whole; and if he uses it then he must maintain the sense, already so strong with Virgil, that each precise heroic event is also something much more—a development of the final and permanent in terms of the immediate and fleeting.

For Virgil and Milton have in common a concept of epic which assumes at the start of the poem the whole course of its action rather than the dominant emotion which is to propel the action as in the case of the *Iliad*. The difference between the wrath of Achilles and man's first disobedience is an epitome of the difference in narrative order between the two poems. One might almost say that, in terms of poetic organization, Homer is telling a story while Milton or Virgil is retelling it.[9]

The significance of this difference for Pope is that he too is retelling a story. He can and in fact must assume some common knowledge of the *Iliad* in his audience, a sort of knowledge quite different from that which the Greeks would have assumed about Achilles. They would have known, of course, the end of Troy which formed the poem's implied climax; but

---

οὐδέ τί πω σάφα ἴδμεν ὅπως ἔσται τάδε ἔργα,
ἢ εὖ ἦε κακῶς νοστήσομεν υἶες Ἀχαιῶν."

"Thersites of reckless speech, clear-voiced talker though you are, refrain, and do not choose to strive singly against kings. . . . We do not at all know clearly yet how these things are to be, whether it be for good or ill that we sons of the Achaeans shall return."

(II, 246–7, 252–3)

8. We see Pope doing so at this point through a metaphysical manipulation of the Greek, where in Chapter II we noticed his particular idea of order as it was developed by the poem's diction.

9. See above, pp. 86–92.

they would not have regarded the detail of the *Iliad* as a part of their prior knowledge of the Troy story. For Pope's society such detail is a part of that prior knowledge, however, just as for Milton the story of the Fall is already present, and for Virgil the myths which associated Rome and Troy.

By this I do not mean to assert that we can be sure how much Homer's audience already knew of his story; but his way of telling it implies both that they knew a great deal about the individual heroes involved and that they did *not* have an elaborate set of prior assumptions about the significance of those heroes for their own culture. Homer's profound concern with the individual and with fate but not with the kinds of human order beween the two indicates that however much his audience knew of Hector or Agamemnon he was free to manipulate them *in terms of the direct action of the poem* as Virgil and Milton were not free to manipulate Aeneas and Adam.

The assumption of prior knowledge which Pope, like them, must make about the story with which he deals, means that like them he reorders it from within in order to make it an instrument of insight for his own society. It becomes a philosophical poem, a poem which in the course of its action meditates on the meaning of the action as Homer never does. Pope's particulars of style and his treatment of the poem's larger narrative meet in this—that both are directed to an interpretation of the *Iliad* as something already known but yet not really known until it is reconsidered in the idiom of Pope's own alien time and place. As a result his version exists at two removes from the simplest epic order, that of *Beowulf* and *The Song of Roland*. Homer differs from them in complexity of action and the insight which results from action; Pope takes the step of speculation and implied generality as well.

Actually such a treatment of the *Iliad* is a test and proof of its vitality; Pope has assimilated it to his own poetic and philosophic world both in its minute particulars and in its total meaning. The conviction with which the poem leaves a reader is that the main action of the *Iliad* is penetrating and revelatory about the life he himself leads. This belief of any discerning critic who has spent time with the original is evoked by means adapted to the reader who will not have that time to spend—who must be excited in his own tongue if he is to be excited at all.

Seen in these terms many objections to the translation assume their proper position of irrelevancy; Pope's *Iliad* is so demonstrably not Homer in one sense that we are free to consider another and perhaps even more important sense in which it "is" Homer. As the last nonsatiric product of the European heroic tradition it maintains against growing opposition the idea that one can look to poetry for an expression of human significance and value. Pope is repaying a debt to Homer by making his own best English the servant of Homer's action, but he will not have made payment unless that action is sustained and informed in every way which allows us to accept its enrichment of our total experience. The shifts and developments between Greek and English are above all ways of making that enrichment available to us.

It must be remembered at the same time, however, that with the inclusion of so much implied critical and philosophic interpretation in the texture of the translation, a dilution of the action results. This is no unjust criticism of Pope but rather a necessary recognition of his dilemma. By the nature of his devotion to Homer he is forced into a sacrifice of the uninterrupted rush of events which is so constantly characteristic of the Greek. It is fair, I think, to say that Pope has done more for the *Iliad* than any other English translator; but in order to insist upon its validity for his own time he has, like every other translator, limited certain aspects of its power. The fact that his interpretation of the *Iliad* develops as a coherent poem saves him from the almost universal translator's fault of merely stating what the original bodies forth or brings to life. But these very qualities which allow us to grant that he has written a heroic poem also force us to grant not only that it is a different poem from Homer's but that as it interprets him it inevitably modifies his driving force.

3

I mentioned a few sentences ago the growing opposition against which Pope must work in his attempt to maintain the living possibility of a major poetic "kind." The nature of that opposition, and of Pope's resistance, is really a reminder both of a turning point in the history of English poetry and of a permanent problem about the nature of poetry itself. For the mathematical universe which in the late seventeenth century began to be regarded as the most real became so in part by denying the value of invention or imagination.

The event is well enough known;[1] what concerns us here is the fact that the best of the Augustans were still struggling against a "dissociation of sensibility." The satiric concern of Pope, Swift, Fielding is among other things an attempt to maintain a moral and spiritual order for the world as opposed to a mathematical order. The writer's vocation comes back so repeatedly as a major theme in Pope's work because he sees bad poetry as the reminder of a potentially ruined society. If we cannot recognize this particular kind of evil when we meet it, we are implying a failure with the other kinds of order which bind the world together.

In Chapter I we saw Pope as a critic aware of this danger. The central

1. In addition to the books mentioned above, p. 98, n. 7, the best statement of changing assumptions is in E. A. Burtt, *The Metaphysical Foundations of Modern Physical Science* (rev. ed. London, Routledge and Kegan Paul, 1949). Eliot's famous discussion of the dissociation of sensibility is in "The Metaphysical Poets," *Selected Essays: 1917-1932*, pp. 241-50.

importance of his concern for imagination and for the support of it by a living poetic tradition lies in his desire to maintain a complex world, a human society at its richest. Pope equates nature and Homer, not nature and the courses of the planets. In doing so he reminds us that poetry is for him a kind of wisdom, a kind of understanding. One cannot separate the poet's world from our "larger" world because the poet is simultaneously making use of it and ordering it.

This use and this order may take many forms; we have seen in the course of the book its two chief aspects—a relation between words which makes them the full realization of a larger event, and a relation between poems which permits the inheritor of a tradition to imply within his poem's action the significance which other actions have already created. In both cases the poet works with the ordinary world and removes himself from it. Achilles is not "real" when we see him as a prophetically doomed warrior at Troy, nor is he literally like a comet as he rushes across the battlefield toward Hector. But precisely because he is not literally presented in either of these ways he can serve as the permanent evocation of despairing and self-frustrated anger.

Descartes's world of "primary" mathematical form serves as a check on the deceptive world of "secondary" physical appearances. The kind of poetry which Pope and Milton support in their different ways also serves as such a check but without losing the value of the immediate, of the actual event. Descartes and Newton generalize from the particular; Milton and Pope mediate between the general and particular but without putting themselves in the paradoxical position of denying the particular from which their general comes. Our curious contemporary bifurcation between the physical world and the world of physics is one logical result of Descartes's separation; the style of Pope or Milton tries constantly to resist this separation by presenting a maximum of immediacy which will also suggest a maximum of generalized significance. The order which we noticed in earlier sections of this chapter is perhaps the largest form of such an attempt. A world picture which depends upon responsible interrelationship is the implied philosophical parallel to a style which, as we noticed in Chapter II, leads among other things to the revelation of man in nature, revealing himself as he participates in his cosmos.

But such a world picture is not a mere historical curiosity; it is something upon which poetry at any time must depend. Pope differs from Homer because Homer's men must war against the world of nature, but the sense of relationship and order is as strong in Homer's Greek as in Pope's English. The place of poetry, and all art, as the meeting point of phenomenon and significance is one which must be fought for at any time. Pope's fight is of particular importance because he is dealing with the early stages of the same opposition to poetry with which we are dealing today. The language which he creates for his translation and its total meaning are ultimately the same thing, an insistence on the primacy of the world of value and an insistence that value can lie neither in mere abstraction nor in raw experience. Value is the concern of metaphor, metaphor recognized as the event which gives meaning—the formal image of a drooping poppy, the sorrowing ineffectuality of Helen as she talks with Hector, Achilles' decision to send Patroclus as a substitute and sacrifice for himself. In each of these we recognize significant experience which by illuminating its own world illuminates ours. In all that he brings to Homer, Pope is concerned with the maintaining of this central quality; and his translation is successful finally in its homage to poetic power. Nature and Homer were, he found, the same; the loss of poetry would be the loss of significant order in the universe. Pope is "faithful" to Homer in maintaining that order at every point; it is the offering of his own fire on the altar of his master.

APPENDIX I

A FULL DISCUSSION of the positive evidence for Pope's knowledge of Greek will be more appropriate in a forthcoming edition of his Homer translations. But because the assumption of his ignorance has been so often and so easily made, I should like to consider briefly some of the common information on the subject which has been either ignored or misconstrued.

During Pope's lifetime there was a good deal of discussion about his knowledge of Greek or lack of it;[1] but the attitude which has been perpetuated seems to stem chiefly from the end of the eighteenth century. Samuel Johnson implied, and Gilbert Wakefield affirmed, that Pope did not know enough of Homer's original to translate directly. Johnson gives his suggestion cogency by indicating how much support he could have had without that central knowledge. One is led to feel that since Pope might have avoided direct contact with Homer, he must have avoided it.[2]

Wakefield's objections are of another sort. The first editor of Pope's Homer is damningly specific about "the strange and scandalous blunders in the typography of the Greek and Latin quotations" and the "fact indubitably certain, that an accurate knowledge of the Greek tongue would have enabled Pope to give us a translation of Homer perfectly precise and faithful, without hazard of evaporation to a single atom from the vital spirit of poetic phrenzy."[3] The sense of every Pope passage, furthermore, can according to him be traced to one of the earlier translations; and one can point to no period of Pope's life when he could have learned Greek adequately.

These objections summarize those which have always been offered as proof of Pope's ignorance of Greek; and in every case there exists an obvious logical or factual objection to such proofs. The scandalous errors in Greek citation which Wakefield finds in Pope's notes, for instance, vanish if one compares his Greek with that in the most learned edition which could have been used by him. A comparison of two-thirds of the quotations with the Greek of Joshuah Barnes' 1711 edition of Homer shows that in almost every case the two agree.[4]

Wakefield failed at this point to recognize that one should compare Pope with what was available to him; but throughout his edition he made the far greater error of assuming that if one knew the Greek he could make a com-

1. See John Dennis, *Critical Works,* ed. E. N. Hooker (Baltimore, 1939–43), II, 124.
A letter from one of Pope's *Odyssey* collaborators to the other expresses similar doubts but is more than countered by earlier exchanges between Pope and his assistants. See D. M. Knight, "Pope's Knowledge of Greek," *Times Literary Supplement,* May 4, 1946, *45*, 211.   2. Johnson, *Lives of the Poets,* III, 113–16.
3. *The Iliad of Homer,* ed. Gilbert Wakefield (London, 1806), I, ccl, cclxxxiii.
4. There is no doubt that Pope and his assistants with the annotation used this edition among others; it was the most recent of the "learned" ones published in England. Barnes is mentioned by name several times in the notes, and remarks are made there which are also in Barnes and certainly not easily available elsewhere (the reference to Porphyry's opinion in Bk. VI, n. xxv, for instance). The errors in Greek, like those in Bk. II, n. vi,

pletely "faithful" poetic translation. In view of the impossibility of such an achievement,[5] it is clearly inaccurate to convict Pope of ignorance on the grounds of his supposed infidelity to the Greek. This is not the place to discuss Wakefield's limitations as an editor, but a glance at a few of his suggested emendations will reveal how easily the theories of a bad critic can destroy the power of a good poem. His changes in the direction of "fidelity" would make complete ruin of any fidelity which parallels the consistent Greek style with a consistent English one.

Such objections suggest what Wakefield's more minor claims about Pope seem to demonstrate—that he started his remarks with the assumption that Pope was a pretender to learning and then set out to produce factual evidence for the assumption. The statement, for instance, that the sense of Pope's version can at every point be traced to an earlier translation depends upon an obvious fallacy. At every point some one of the earlier translations will be close to Homer's sense; is it just to claim that if Pope is also close he must be following the earlier translator? Wakefield never produces evidence to show that Pope deviates *from* Homer at the beckoning of some earlier translation; and as Appendix II demonstrates Pope was quite surprisingly independent from his predecessors in the choice of word and phrase. What he shared with them was mainly the penumbra of possible meaning which stems from any given passage of Homer.

The biographical problem of a time when Pope might have learned Greek raises a question of definition. How well must Pope learn it in order to be qualified as a translator? Certainly it is obvious that he was not a professionally learned man, but Wakefield and others have assumed from his lack of formal education that he must be an ignorant man.[6] His formally educated friends seem not to have noticed this ignorance, however,[7] and if we accept the evidence of his work it implies a wide and subtly understood range of knowledge somewhat like that of Shakespeare, a poet equally informal in his education. His specific aptitude for languages was well known in the family,[8] and he himself remarked in private conversation on a certain period of his late childhood as that which was chiefly occupied with reading in Latin and Greek.[9]

In a correspondence of 1708 over his first attempts at translating Homer, Pope confesses to his friend Ralph Bridges that he was misled by Chapman and Hobbes in his version of a certain passage. This remark is often produced to show how badly Pope must have been fumbling, but a look at the

---

where Pope has πέτωνται for πέτονται and πε ποτήαται for πεποτήαται, are minor enough to suggest no more than that he was textually ill informed at times.

5. See above, pp. 1–6.

6. W. J. Courthope, for instance, in his *Life of Alexander Pope* (London, 1889), p. 166, accepts Wakefield's listing of errors and remarks casually that "it is indeed sufficiently obvious that Pope did not understand the Greek text."

7. The excellent account of Pope's education in Sherburn, *Early Career*, suggests several reasons why it was more adequate than a devotee of the English Public School system like Courthope could ever realize.

8. Joseph Spence, *Anecdotes, Observations, and Characters, of Books and Men*, ed. S. W. Singer (London, 1858), pp. 19–20.   9. *Ibid.*, pp. 204, 211.

original correspondence suggests some other things as well.[1] Pope was certainly feeling his way; these letters were written five years before his serious work of translation began, and he was unsure of himself. But nevertheless he discussed with Bridges the Greek of the passages, not the virtues of the earlier translators—who are actually mentioned only in a casual way. And, though it is a minor matter, the lines of Greek written by him during the correspondence are in a well-formed and obviously assured hand.[2]

Like a later letter to William Broome in which Pope says that he has already translated some notes from Eustathius,[3] this correspondence suggests a more plausible view of Pope's knowledge than one which assumes his mere ignorance. He had learned a fair amount of Greek but was properly aware that it was not complete command. He admitted his hesitations and got all the help he honorably could. He was not a *poseur,* though he was not a professional Greek scholar; all the circumstantial evidence which we have points to his honesty about this position and suggests that it gave him a legitimate right to deal with Homer's poem in the terms which he chose as his own—those of a poet embodying in his own poetic idiom the major works of an alien language.

1. The exchange of questions is bound in with Vol. 1 of the Pope Homer manuscripts in the British Museum, Add. Ms. 4807, folios 194r–198v.
2. Spence, *Anecdotes,* p. 201.
3. See *The Works of Alexander Pope,* eds. Elwin and Courthope, VIII, 35.

APPENDIX II

IN ADDITION to translations of the whole *Iliad* by Chapman, Ogilby, and Hobbes (for which see above, p. 24 n. 6), Pope had available to him the French version of Mme. Dacier, first published in 1699, and the English translation of her French by Ozell (see above, p. 25, n. 5). There were many fragmentary translations, of course; the two which seem valuable for Book 1 are Dryden's version of the whole book, which appeared in the 1700 edition of the *Fables,* and Manwaring's of the first two-thirds, which appeared in *Poetical Miscellanies: The Fifth Part* . . . (London, 1704), pp. 456–83.

I have listed the important similarities between Pope and the earlier translators in the following form: line number in the first edition of Pope's *Iliad;* name of earlier translator; quotation of pertinent words or phrases. Two things are striking about the list: its indication of precise verbal similarities between various translations, which are much more obvious in Book 1 than later in the poem; and its equally clear indication that there were no sustained stylistic developments of the *Iliad* in English upon which Pope could have depended.

Book I

1	Dryden	the wrath of Peleus' son
2	Ogilby	great goddess, sing
3	Dacier	dans le sobre royaume de Pluton
5	Manwaring	whose limbs
6	Ogilby	devouring vultures
		greedy dogs
	Dacier	aux chiens et aux vautours
11	Ozell	Latona's son . . . spread
	Manwaring	fair Latona's son
13	Chapman	the king of men
	Dryden	the king of men
14	Ogilby	the people die
17	Dryden	the venerable father
		suppliant before
18	Dryden	Awful, and armed with ensigns of his God
20	Dryden	laurel crown
29	Dacier	ces présents
31	Ozell	shouts
38	Ozell	those vain ensigns of the God thou serv'st
43	Hobbes	and labour at the loom
46	Dryden	far from . . . her native home
	Dacier	à Argos, loin de sa patrie
	Ozell	far from her native country
47	Manwaring	the trembling priest

50	Manwaring	in silent [passion]
	Ozell	silently
54	Manwaring	thou guardian king
55	Dryden	source of sacred light
	Manwaring	thou glorious light
57	Chapman	thy rich fane
	Ogilby	thy fane
58	Chapman	fat thighs of oxen
59	Manwaring	with thy silver bow
67	Hobbes	the bow was heard to twang
	Manwaring	a deadly dart
		the twang was dreadful
	Ozell	the bow-string twang'd
68	Dacier	un sifflement
74	Dacier	inspire
76	Manwaring	for much the . . . goddess
77	Dacier	assembles [sic] (Cf. "une assemble" for Pope's "Council," 75.)
81	Ozell	sword and pestilence
86	Hobbes	For also dreams descend on men from Jove
	Manwaring	(dreams from Jove descend)
	Ozell	(for dreams proceed from *Jove*)
87	Manwaring	or broken vows
88	Dacier	des hécatombes promises
94	Dacier	le présent, le passé, et l'avenir
	Manwaring	And knew the present, past, and things to come
	Ozell	things past, and present, and to come
96	Dacier	as prudence
97	Chapman	Jove's beloved
	Manwaring	best belov'd of Jove
104	Manwaring	a monarch
108	Dryden	And speak without control
111	Manwaring	celestial oracles . . . declare
112	Dryden	while my nostrils draw this vital air
117	Ogilby	the blameless prophet
	Manwaring	encouraged thus, the blameless
118	Chapman	not unpaid vows
	Dryden	nor vows unpaid
	Dacier	ni de vos voeux, ni de vos sacrifices
	Manwaring	not broken vows
		nor sacrifice unpaid
120	Dryden	in his injured priest
	Ozell	his priest, injured
124	Chapman	the black-eyed damsel
	Manwaring	the black-eyed maid
128	Dryden	upstarting from his throne
129-30	Dryden	His breast with fury filled, his eyes with fire
	Ogilby	his breast with choler burnt

	Manwaring	Black choler boiling in his manly breast
138	Dryden	in his priest profan'd
144	Dryden	in beauty's bloom
146	Manwaring	The publick safety is my only care
151	Manwaring	the fair
155	Ozell	insatiate
161	Manwaring	nor you resume
165	Manwaring	whene'er, by Jove's decree
170	Manwaring	think not to . . . my right
179	Dryden	or aloud complain
180	Ozell	let him rage
185	Dryden	the fair
	Manwaring	my . . . fair
187	Dryden	Creta's king
192	Ozell	and grow propitious
193	Manwaring	Achilles frowning
	Ogilby	frowning on him, stern Achilles
194	Dacier	l'insolence
	Manwaring	with insolence
	Ozell	whose insolence
198	Dacier	en ambuscade
	Manwaring	to march in ambush
199	Manwaring	no cause had I
200	Manwaring	the distant Trojans
	Ogilby	The warlike Trojans never injured me
	Ozell	Nor did the Trojans ever injure me
205	Manwaring	fruitful Pthia
213	Manwaring	my prize
217–18	Dryden	prey
		day
218	Chapman	fruit of my sweat
	Manwaring	mine is the toil and danger
228	Manwaring	and Jove himself
229	Dryden	of all the kings
	Manwaring	of all the kings
230	Manwaring	none to my power
231	Ozell	debates
234	Ozell	thy valour
245–6	Manwaring	So will I seize Briseis in thy tent
248	Dacier	plus de pouvoir
251	Dacier	de douleur et de rage
255	Ozell	draw his sword
256	Ozell	forcing the guard
261	Manwaring	from above
	Ozell	Minerva descended from above
263	Manwaring	(For both the princes shar'd her equal love;)
264	Dacier	par les cheveux
	Manwaring	Behind she stood . . . hair

268	Chapman	sparkling
	Dryden	by her sparkling eyes
	Manwaring	sparkling eyes
	Ogilby	sparkling of her dreadful eyes
272	Dryden	to view the vengeance
279	Dacier	des reproches
294	Dryden	senate
298	Manwaring	a flying deer
	Ogilby	hearted like a deer
308	Hobbes	had been your last
	Ozell	this day would be the last
309–10	Dryden	But by this sceptre solemnly I swear,
		(Which never more green leaf or growing branch shall bear . . .)
	Manwaring	But by this awful sceptre now I swear,
		(Which ne'er again will happy branches bear . . .)
311	Dacier	séparé du tronc
315	Dacier	les lois et la justice
322	Manwaring	thy impotence
324	Manwaring	the bravest Greek
326	Chapman	golden studs
	Manwaring	golden studs
	Ogilby	golden studs
332	Dryden	Words, sweet as honey, from his mouth distilled
	Manwaring	words flowed like honey
	Ogilby	sweeter than honey
	Ozell	sweeter from his mouth, than honey
333	Manwaring	two generations
	Ozell	had seen two ages pass
339	Manwaring	what . . . woes . . . what . . . joys
	Ozell	what . . . woe . . . what . . . joy
345	Manwaring	a race of heroes
346	Dacier	je ne verray jamais
355	Manwaring	Strongest of men
358	Ozell	to be swayed
359	Manwaring	when your Nestor spoke
367	Manwaring	born of a goddess
375	Manwaring	our strongest bulwark
	Ogilby	like a strong bulwark
377	Ozell	thy words are wise
381	Ozell	His will's a law
386	Manwaring	Achilles broke
388	Manwaring	deserv'd thy galling yoke
391	Ozell	Command thy slaves, not me
406	Ogilby	fair Chruseis
407	Manwaring	with command was graced
		ploughed

409	Manwaring	the liquid road
414	Dacier	des hécatombes
414–15	Manwaring	whole hecatombs
		fat bulls and goats
	Ozell	most perfect hecatombs of bulls and goats
418	Ogilby	sacred rites
427	Dryden	barren shore
	Ogilby	barren shore
429	Dryden	upon his hand reclined
432	Ozell	their confusion
435	Dacier	sacres ministres des dieux et des hommes
	Ozell	ye sacred ministers of gods and men
440–1	Dacier	témoins devant les dieux et devant
		les hommes
	Manwaring	that each a witness
	Ozell	be you my witnesses
441	Manwaring	and gods above
446–7	Manwaring	lost
		host
450	Manwaring	an unwilling heart
462	Chapman	so short a life
462–4	Chapman	my short life honor
	Ogilby	My short life Jove should lengthen out in fame
468	Manwaring	in the deepest Main
471	Manwaring	strait like a mist she rose
	Ozell	like a mist
474–5	Manwaring	And said, why weeps my son? Thy grief declare,
		And let thy tender parent bear her share
478	Dacier	la sacrée ville de Thèbes
	Ozell	Eetion's sacred city
495	Manwaring	and Phoebus heard him
498	Chapman	prophet
	Hobbes	prophet
	Manwaring	a prophet then
502–3	Chapman	used threats, performed
	Dryden	the swelling monarch storm'd
		perform'd
	Hobbes	what he threatened
	Manwaring	who loudly stormed
		To threaten vengeance, which he since perform'd
	Ogilby	stormed,
		And what he saying threatened, hath performed
514–15	Manwaring	in Thessalia boast
		of all th'aetherial host
523	Ogilby	Whom gods Briereus, men Ægaeon call
531	Chapman	embrace his knee
	Dacier	en embrassant ses genoux
	Manwaring	embrace his knees

	Ozell	embrace his knees
533	Manwaring	on the main
	Ogilby	drive them to the main
544–5	Ozell	so short . . . not only short, but full of sorrow too
551	Chapman	Olympus crowned with snow
552	Dryden	secure in ships
557	Chapman	the blameless Æthiops
	Dryden	blameless Æthiops
	Ozell	the blameless Æthiopians
568	Hobbes	his sails he furled
	Ogilby	and lash their mast
	Ozell	the sails are furl'd
591	Dacier	la divine Cilla
601	Dacier	la teste vers le ciel
604	Ogilby	a double cawl
609	Dryden	the youth
610	Ozell	the entrails
615	Dacier	des libations
619	Chapman	and spent in paeans to the sun
620	Ozell	nor ungrateful
623	Dryden	rosy morn
636	Dacier	conseils, ni aux combats
642	Dryden	ascending
651	Dacier	embrassant ses genoux
	Dryden	one hand embraced his knees
	Ozell	did embrace his sacred knees
680	Hobbes	a nod
	Ogilby	with a nod
681	Dacier	irrevocable
	Dryden	irrevocable
684	Chapman	th'ambrosian curls
	Dryden	ambrosial dews
	Ozell	th'ambrosial locks
708	Chapman	what fits
	Hobbes	you first of all shall know
713	Ozell	majestic
714	Chapman	austere
729	Dacier	odieuse
	Ozell	odious
731	Dacier	et ce qu'il doit estre
	Ozell	and ought to be
741	Dryden	architect
753	Dryden	crown'd a bowl unbid
758	Dryden	I dare not aid
774	Dacier	Apollon jouait de la lyre
	Ozell	Apollo touched the lyre
781	Ogilby	Fair Juno by him on a golden bed

Index

YALE STUDIES IN ENGLISH

This volume is the one hundred and seventeenth of the Yale Studies in English, founded by Albert Stanburrough Cook in 1898 and edited by him until his death in 1927. Tucker Brooke succeeded him as editor, and served until 1941, when Benjamin C. Nangle succeeded him.

The following volumes are still in print. Orders should be addressed to YALE UNIVERSITY PRESS, New Haven, Connecticut.